twilight

THE COMPLETE ILLUSTRATED MOVIE COMPANION

BY MARK COTTA VAZ

www.atombooks.co.uk

ATOM

Copyright © 2008 by Hachette Book Group
Unless otherwise credited, all photographs copyright © 2008 by Summit Entertainment, LLC

The moral right of the author has been asserted.

All characters and events in this publication, other than
those clearly in the public domain, are fictitious
and any resemblance to real persons,
living or dead, is purely coincidental.

A CIP catalogue record for this book
is available from the British Library.

First Atom UK/ANZ Edition 2008

ISBN 978-1-905654-42-0

Printed and bound in the UK by Butler Tanner & Dennis Ltd, Frome

Atom
An imprint of
Little, Brown Book Group
100 Victoria Embankment
London EC4Y 0DY

An Hachette Livre UK Company
www.hachettelivre.co.uk

www.atombooks.co.uk

Edward and Bella were

falling in love. There was nothing remarkable
about that, nor that the two teenagers
would be sitting outside at dusk, talking
and watching the rain and darkening sky.
A passerby might have been struck by the
young man's good looks, but the scene was
otherwise innocent and ordinary. But the two
teens shared a secret—Edward was a vampire.

"It's twilight," Edward noted. "It's the safest
time for us. The easiest time. But also the
saddest, in a way . . . the end of another
day, the return of the night. Darkness is
so predictable, don't you think?"

"I like the night," Bella replied. "Without
the dark, we'd never see the stars."[1]

TABLE OF CONTENTS

Forbidden Love

Everything you know about vampires is wrong.

That classic image of a ruined castle atop a craggy peak and a dark passageway within leading to a cobwebbed crypt where vampires slumber in coffins from dawn to dusk? Wrong. That business about vampires being nocturnal, able to transform into bats, and for whom it's death to be caught in sunlight? Not true. The power of a crucifix or garlic cloves to ward off the undead? Don't even go there.

Imagine instead a cultured family of vampires who commune with mortals in the daytime, drive fast cars, never sleep, and include a respected member of the community. Imagine a scenario in which vampires avoid sunlight only because it reveals their true nature to humans—a vampire's pale skin reflects sunshine like the light of a thousand sparkling diamonds. Imagine the "cold ones" as an evolved species, their genesis lost in the primordial mystery of prehistory. Forget the fanged nocturnal bloodsuckers of legend and see vampires for what they really are—beautiful creatures.

Such are the revisionist takes on vampire lore posited by Stephenie Meyer in *Twilight*, her debut novel published in 2005. The story is told from the point of view of seventeen-year-old Isabella Swan, whose parents are divorced and who has just moved from her mom's house in the Phoenix suburb of Scottsdale to her dad's home in Forks, Washington, a small town in the Olympic Peninsula perpetually shrouded in rainy weather. For Bella, as she prefers to be called, it's a return to where she has spent most of her summers and a place she detests but her father, the chief of police, has always loved. She enrolls at Forks High School and quickly notices the Cullen kids, the children of a local respected doctor. They're hard to miss—they dress and look like fashion models, and Edward Cullen, Bella's partner in biology class, is the

most handsome of all. No one suspects they're vampires. As Bella grows closer to Edward and discovers his secrets, she learns Dr. Carlisle Cullen's coven has made the choice to feed on wild animals, not human blood—"vegetarian vampires," they joke. One rare sun-filled day, Edward reveals himself to Bella by showing his skin shimmering in the sunlight, exhibiting his physical strength and speed, and describing his instinct for human blood—and she loves him all the more. Edward has found his soul mate in Bella, but he's tortured by her intoxicating scent and has to resist making his love his prey. Bella sees Edward as a pillar of strength, with a face and body like a Renaissance marble figure come to life—"Edward…glorious as a young god," she sighs—and she's so in love she begins flirting with the notion that Edward should take her and make her a vampire so they can spend eternity together.[2]

Twilight left readers with Bella and Edward poised on that razor's edge of desire. The book became a *New York Times* bestselling phenomenon and the saga continued with *New Moon*, *Eclipse*, and *Breaking Dawn*. The first book caught Hollywood's interest, and an adaptation

of *Twilight*, directed by Catherine Hardwicke and released by Summit Entertainment, was ready to roll into theaters.

The idea that started it all came to Meyer in a dream, the means by which many great artistic creations have come into the world. The doomed Dr. Frankenstein and his monster, for example, came to life in the hypnogogic vision of nineteen-year-old Mary Wollstonecraft Godwin (soon to be Shelley). She had seen "the pale student of unhallowed arts," repulsed by the first sign of life from the man-thing he had constructed, flee to his bedroom, where he prayed it would sink back into "dead matter." But when he opened his eyes, he saw his terrible creation pulling back his bed curtains.[3]

There's the strange case of writer Robert Louis Stevenson, whose sickly childhood and fevered sleep was haunted by a "night-hag" from which the only escape was to awaken, screaming. By adulthood, Stevenson claimed to have harnessed that "speechless midnight fear" for his storytelling, with "the little people…the Brownies," as he called them, providing his slumbering mind with marketable ideas. Such was the night when his wife awakened him as he cried out in his sleep. With some irritation at her interruption, Stevenson told her, "I was dreaming a fine bogey tale." His nightmare became *Dr. Jekyll and Mr. Hyde*.[4]

Unlike the pomp and flash of Shelley's Romantic era clique and Stevenson's lifelong fevers, Stephenie Meyer's life did not portend vampiric dreams. She was born in Connecticut in 1973, but by age four her family relocated to Phoenix. She and her siblings were neatly divided, three boys and three girls, Stephenie being the second of the girls. As a teenager she attended high school in tony Scottsdale, "the kind of place where every fall a few girls would come back to school with new noses and there were Porsches in the student lot," she recalls. She won a National Merit Scholarship that paid her way as an English major at Brigham Young University, a school that "consistently and proudly" finishes last on lists of the nation's party schools, Meyer notes with satisfaction. She had known her future husband as an acquaintance from that first year her family arrived in Phoenix, but it took sixteen years before the whirlwind courtship that led to marriage and, more than ten years later, three sons.

Everything changed for Meyer the night a vivid dream took her to a forest meadow where she saw an average-looking girl and a stunningly handsome vampire having an intense conversation. "Confessions," the thirteenth chapter of *Twilight*, is "essentially a transcript of my dream," Meyer has revealed.[5] Meyer can pinpoint that dream date, the day *Twilight* was born—June 2, 2003—because when she awakened it was the first day of swimming lessons for her boys. Throughout that day she was haunted

THE DAY *Twilight* WAS BORN— JUNE 2, 2003

Twilight author Stephenie Meyer on the laptop... in her cameo role

and compelled to write the story of those two oddly paired characters in the meadow. In a sense, she never awakened from her dream.

The lore and legend of vampires stretches into antiquity, with practically every culture having some mythic notion of the creatures, often tortured souls who drink the blood of their victims. But the modern fascination with vampires can be traced to a stormy night over Lake Geneva, Switzerland, and a villa that had become refuge to Lord George Gordon Byron, the handsome, brilliant poet who was driven there from England by scandals befitting his notorious appetites and melancholic musings. This particular night, while a torrential downpour raged outside, Byron, along with the aforementioned Mary W. Godwin; her lover and future husband, the poet Shelley; and one Dr. John Polidori, spent the midnight hours exchanging tales of horror and the supernatural, and agreed to a contest to see who could write the best such story. In posterity's judgment Mary won with *Frankenstein*, but Polidori produced *The Vampyre*, published anonymously in 1819 but ascribed to the brooding Byron, whose own doomed, dark, and romantic nature had "the vampire image" about him.

From that villa in Switzerland, the years saw many a vampire-based theatrical play and magic lantern show, until Bram Stoker's novel *Dracula* in 1897, which has within its narrative DNA the bloody rule of fifteenth-century warlord Vlad III, who lived in a castle in Transylvania and whose reign included having

hundreds of Turkish prisoners of war impaled on spikes. Vlad's crest featured a dragon that in the regional tongue also meant devil—*dracul*.[6] And then, in a new century, moving pictures allowed the conjuring of ever more haunting versions of the undead, notably actor Béla Lugosi's aristocratic Count Dracula.

For *Twilight* director Catherine Hardwicke, the creative journey of the movie adaptation included retracing this path of legend into the realms of vampire lore around the world. "One reason the *Twilight* series has such resonance may be that the vampire myth is deeply rooted in the human psyche," Hardwicke said. "A wide array of ancient cultures have vampire myths—from Indonesia to China to Egypt to South America. Many tales describe women who have lost babies or have died in childbirth, then roam the earth at night wreaking havoc on the living. Some are deliciously gruesome and designed to keep children indoors. Fourteenth-century Romanian government documents give detailed accounts of vampire grave openings. Even the practice of cremation may have been motivated by the desire to keep the dead from returning to the realm of the living. I found blueprints for a specialized coffin with a built-in device—a stake would stab the corpse's heart if [it] tried to escape."

There have been theories as to why the vampire myth managed to burrow itself deep into humanity's collective consciousness. Joel Schumacher, who directed *The Lost Boys*, a film about vampires haunting a resort town on the California coast, puts one compelling notion best: "I think one of the reasons vampires have an enduring quality is they're the only monsters that are really sexy."[7]

And therein lies the special attraction of *Twilight*.

"There have been [hundreds] of vampire movies, but I never thought of *Twilight* as a vampire movie," said Greg Mooradian, the film producer who discovered *Twilight*. "The vampires are really nothing more than a hook, the vehicle to tell the story of forbidden love."

Looking for a book with potential to be a movie "property" was always the proverbial search for a needle in a haystack, Mooradian noted. A book scout in New York brought him *Twilight* when it was still a raw manuscript being edited by Megan Tingley at Little, Brown and Company. "There is no way to predict the life of a book. You have to go with your instinct. Often, when I'm reading a young adult book, I have to imagine whether a fifteen-year-old girl might enjoy reading it. What struck me in my initial reading of the *Twilight* manuscript was how much *I* enjoyed it, how completely absorbing it was, even while knowing I was far afield of who the book was supposed to speak to. My reaction told me this was more than a book for young girls. This was a first-time author's unedited novel, but I was able to see past [its raw quality] because the themes of the story and the

"I NEVER THOUGHT OF *Twilight* AS A VAMPIRE MOVIE."

characters were so wonderful. It had universal themes, like *Romeo and Juliet*, which certainly influenced this book. It struck me this was a great movie premise—it seemed the greatest idea nobody had ever done. But, at the time there was no way to predict it would connect with every young girl in America the way it has, that it would become an anthem for young girls as much as anything in contemporary culture."

Mooradian brought *Twilight* to Karen Rosenfelt, president of production at Paramount. "Greg was so passionate, and ready to dive on his sword, knowing this would be a franchise both for publishing and for film," Rosenfelt recalled.

The project was optioned by Paramount's MTV Films in April 2004 and a writer was hired to produce a screenplay. But complications ensued—Paramount was shaken by what Mooradian calls "an absolute changing of the guard," which included the departure of production head Rosenfelt. In the process *Twilight* "got caught" in limbo when a new regime took over, Rosenfelt recalled. "It languished." But the book soon became a publishing phenomenon— *Twilight* wouldn't be languishing for long.

"*Twilight* taps into that young girl's primacy of first love and forbidden love, and how much more forbidden is it than to fall in love with a vampire? Bella herself is accessible to girls. Bella captures the side we all have, that feeling of being an outsider looking in while still trying to keep our iconoclastic nature."

—KAREN ROSENFELT

"Edward loves Bella and wants to protect her, that's everybody's fantasy. And there's sexual tension. They can't go too far or he'll kill her, which is this tingling, exhilarating thing! It's temptation and desire… We're trying to convey a great love story about this girl, a heightened passion, and that first love where you'll do anything. Who doesn't remember writing the person's name 8,000 times in the notebook and watching and figuring and planning every minute as to how you'd get a glimpse of that person at school, where even if they brush by you in the hall it's magic! All that stuff Stephenie conveys."

—CATHERINE HARDWICKE

Meanwhile, Summit Entertainment, a film company which for some twenty years specialized in foreign distribution and co-financing productions, was making the move to become a full-fledged studio and looking for potential projects. "*Twilight* got out of its limbo state because Greg as a producer was so extraordinarily passionate about it and always beating the drums on it," Rosenfelt recalled. "I had a meeting with Erik Feig, the president at Summit, and he asked me if there was any project he should chase down that Paramount might let go. I told him the one he should get hold of is *Twilight*."

At that point, Paramount's rights were about to expire. Summit pursued it, and secured the rights in February of 2006. It has since become "a flagship project" for Summit, notes Rosenfelt (who is a credited executive producer on the final film).

Twilight the movie really got rolling when it came to the attention of director Catherine Hardwicke, whose credits included being a production designer on such films as the 2001 release *Vanilla Sky*, which Summit had distributed, and whose directorial debut was *Thirteen* in 2003 followed by *The Lords of Dogtown* (2005). Hardwicke recalls that when she was on the competition jury of the Sundance film festival in 2007 she met and had dinner with Summit executives Patrick Wachsberger and Erik Feig. "They were very friendly and said they admired

LONG PASSAGES OF TEXT WHERE BELLA DESCRIBES THE BEAUTY OF EDWARD'S FACE COULD BE SUMMED UP IN A SINGLE SHOT.

Thirteen. Apparently, they had almost helped finance it, and regretted that they didn't. Erik said, 'It was the one that got away.' He invited me to come meet with them and see if we could make a film together."

The script that jumped out was *Twilight*, although it was the early version developed at Paramount's MTV Films. "*Twilight* was fascinating to me, but on the opening page, Bella is introduced as a star athlete, she's like a track star," Hardwicke recalled. "Bella is clumsy! She's not an athlete, she's awkward. She's like every other girl, that's why we relate to her. By the end of that script it was like Charlie's Angels, with the FBI and jet skis. I said to Summit, 'You guys have to make it like the book.' So, we went back to Stephenie's book."

It was the logical move, Greg Mooradian agreed, as the novel was no longer an unknown quantity and neither was its author. "Why mess with something that was absolutely working in its own right? By the time Summit became involved there was no question about adhering to the novel."

The mantra of the movie makers was to be faithful to the novel. Meyer, who approved the final screenplay (by Melissa Rosenberg), also saw the advantage of the old adage of a picture being worth a thousand words—long passages of text where Bella describes the beauty of Edward's face could be summed up in a single shot, for example. "We just took the book into

film language," Hardwicke explained. "The novel had to go through the condensing machine for a movie; we had to boil it down to its essence. In a movie we can show more action, so my goal was to make it a little less internal. If there was a passive scene, we tried to find ways to make it visually active. Stephenie gave us a lot of awesome notes; she has a feeling for things Bella would feel and say better than anyone else. In the screenplay, Stephenie also got to address tiny technical things she might have changed in her first novel… But [as in the book], we only convey Bella's point of view; the film only sees what she sees."

Casting was a challenge, as the legion of *Twilight* fans had their own notions and mental pictures of the characters on the printed page. The casting couldn't be done in a vacuum, as the two leads playing Bella Swan and Edward Cullen had to have an onscreen chemistry to match their literary counterparts. The first to be cast, Mooradian recalls, was Kristen Stewart, whose roles ranged from *Panic Room* to *Into the Wild* and who was exactly Bella's age during most of the filming. Although Mooradian had been excited by Kristen's casting, he remembers Robert Pattinson—best known as Cedric Diggory in *Harry Potter and the Goblet of Fire*—as "more of a dark horse." But Pattinson went after the part and won them over. "He went above and beyond," Mooradian recalls of the actor's personal work in getting under Edward's skin and becoming the character.

Greg Mooradian stayed on as a producer from the film's preproduction prep work through postproduction. During principal photography, he was at the shooting location as much as possible, but his time was split with another

Director Catherine Hardwicke

project in Los Angeles. Hardwicke called upon veteran producer Wyck Godfrey, who had been a producer on Hardwicke's *The Nativity Story* (2006), to be involved in the day-to-day work of principal photography.

When Godfrey came aboard, the production was gearing up for a challenging location shoot. Godfrey, who had experience with book projects adapted to movies, approved of the production's decision to be faithful to the novel. "When Catherine contacted me I read the *Twilight* novel and the script in December [of 2007]. The great thing was they stayed almost slavishly faithful to the book. I believe you start with your base, make sure they're happy, and then you can expand outward. Straying from a book doesn't inspire the most confidence from fans. In the case of *Twilight*, Stephenie Meyer was involved in the development of the script—I noticed that immediately! If this is such a beloved book, it's beloved for a reason, so let's make a movie of that book, not just another vampire movie.

"Part of the draw for me was to work with Catherine again," Godfrey added. "She is a very visual person. When we're talking something through, it's almost easier for her to sketch it out. That ability is so helpful to a producer because, whether it's polished or not, you can see what she's going for. She'll even go to her own closet and bring out fabrics to show the costume designer—she's got that level of detail. But Catherine was the perfect choice to direct *Twilight* because her movies always capture the emotional truth of adolescence, the rawness of that experience. What separates this from other genre movies is it's raw, emotional, and you feel a true love story taking place."

"The thing I liked about the world Stephenie Meyer created was it asked you to take one fantastical leap when you walked in the door—vampires live among us and we don't know it. [The] rest of the story is grounded in the real world and allowed me to enjoy the fantastical element all the more."

—GREG MOORADIAN

Bella visits a bookstore set,
created in St. Helens, OR.

"If what you're seeing is real, it's going to feel real."

— CATHERINE HARDWICKE

Hardwicke brought unusual skills to *Twilight*. She grew up in McAllen, a South Texas town straddling the Mexican border, and in the 1980s graduated from the University of Texas at Austin with her five-year professional architect's degree. Hardwicke notes she built some one hundred buildings in South Texas and points with satisfaction to a complex of 120 townhouses she designed in every particular, from a three-acre lake to landscaping and a "passive solar" approach that oriented structures to take advantage of the sun and prevailing wind. But that project was an exception. "Architecture is conservative by nature. It costs a lot of money, it's permanent, and clients are worried about resale value. And then, clients just wanted me to keep repeating the same look. After one lady asked me to switch the position of her water heater with her washing machine for the third time, I applied

Director Catherine Hardwicke on the set of the biology classroom with Kristen Stewart and Robert Pattinson

to UCLA Film School in the graduate film program, specializing in animation.

"One night I was dancing at a club in Hollywood and met a producer, Allan Sacks, who was making a skateboard movie called *Thrashin'*. Since I used to be an architect, he thought that maybe I could 'production design' his movie. My budget was five thousand for the art department. My crew crashed on my floor or in the art truck in hammocks. We used an abandoned crack house as our bad guys' location and got threatened by Venice gang members for graffitiing over their tags. But I was hooked. The biggest difference from my architectural thinking was an architect designs everything to be pristine and clean and beautiful, but when you're designing for a film you're trying to make a statement about a character—how they live and breathe, their habits and history. An orange shag rug might have horrified me as an architect if someone put it into a house I had designed, but as a production designer, I might find it was the exact thing to tell the character's story. I started falling in love with peeling paint and newspapers stuffed into cracks."

In addition to being faithful to the book, the director's preference for shooting in real places was another guiding principle. "I've been trained to imagine things in a visual way," Hardwicke reflected. "How much depth can you get, how much story can you tell by having real locations and dressing the set in a way that

feels we're in a real person's bedroom, that a real person lives there?"

Although a digital camera was tested in preproduction by effects crews, the production shot with regular film. The world of *Twilight*, although having undeniable fantasy elements, would not be a "greenscreen" show, with actors performing on soundstages in front of the neutral backings that allow for the subsequent addition of computer generated environments. "My feeling is CGI [computer graphics imagery] is best used sparingly," Hardwicke said. "If you have a practical [real] setting you don't need that CG look. Maybe you only need one little magical thing in the corner, and three quarters of the frame is real. If what you're seeing is real, it's going to feel real."

Her director of photography (DP), Elliot Davis, had filmed not only Hardwicke's first film but also her 2005 release *Lords of Dogtown* and *The Nativity Story*. *Twilight* department heads and crew included other veterans of Hardwicke's productions. Makeup artist Jeanne Van Phue and hair stylist Mary Ann Valdes had worked on *Dogtown*, location manager James Lin had scouted for *The Monkey Wrench Gang*, a film Hardwicke hopes to make, and set decorator Gene Serdena counted twenty years of their working together.

Director of Photography Elliot Davis

Twilight would have visual effects work— some 250 shots' worth—with visual effects supervisor Richard Kidd and a team from his LA-based company, Catalyst Media, that included his producer, Petra Holtorf, overseeing the work, with CIS Vancouver and Industrial Light + Magic (ILM), the famed visual effects house that began with *Star Wars*, contributing key shots. The bits of movie magic would be done "in-camera" as much as possible, with Andy Weder (fresh from special effects foreman duties on *Pirates of the Caribbean: At World's End*) supervising the special effects, and Hong Kong action veteran Kai Chung Cheng, who goes by "Andy" Cheng, serving as stunt coordinator and second unit director.

As with all productions, the assemblage of cast and crew generated its own unique chemistry. Each person in this most collaborative of artistic mediums brought his or her own special expertise, and each had personal experiences and tales to tell. The work itself, divided into preproduction, principal photography and postproduction, reflected the shrinking timelines of modern movie making. From the time Hardwicke pulled out that old *Twilight* script at the Summit offices, the production was on a fast track to a forty-five-day principal photography shoot that began in March of 2008. By the time filming wrapped and Hardwicke returned to Los Angeles to begin postproduction, the theatrical release date was bearing down like an oncoming bullet train.

It would be a tough shoot, with filming planned for the actual places described in the novel. At one point, Hardwicke asked Meyer why she had set her story in the Pacific Northwest, specifically that small town in Washington called Forks. "The vampires seek out places where there's the least amount of sunlight," Hardwicke noted, "so Stephenie did research to find the rainiest place in the continental United States, the place with the least sunshine year round—and that's Forks!"

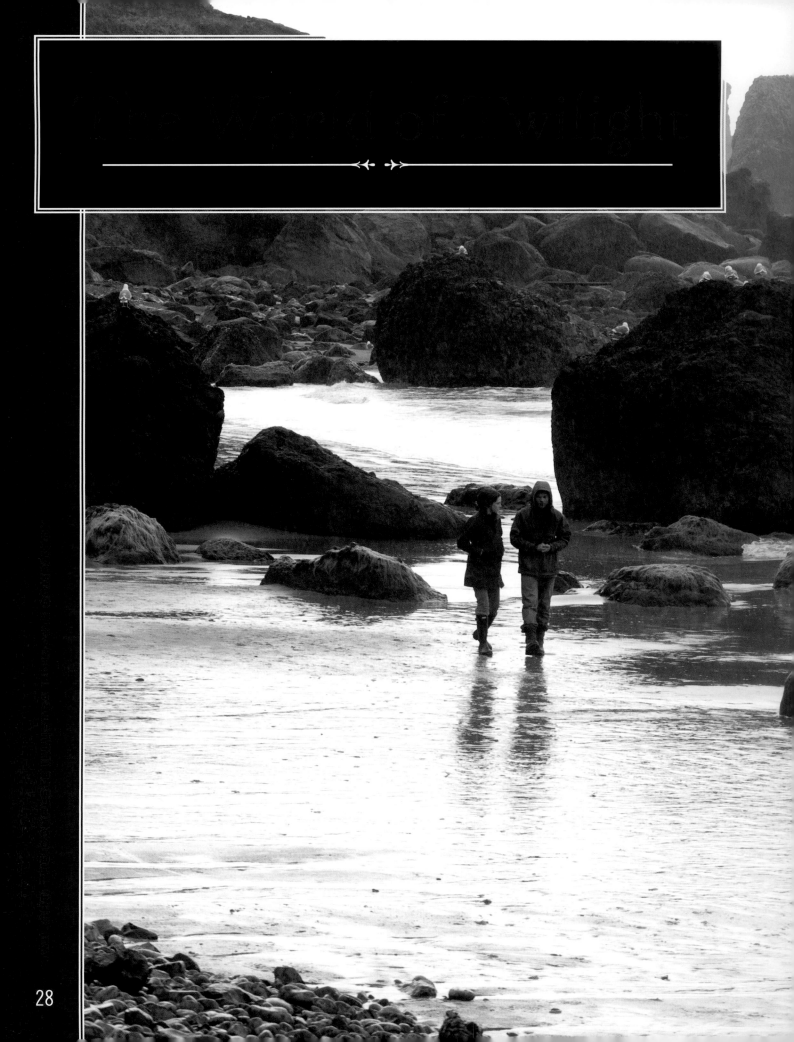

The World of Twilight

*First Street,
St. Helens, OR,
substituting as
Port Angeles, WA*

The Olympia rain forest region is a photographic dream, with ancient trees and mossy growth, soaring mountains, rocky coast, and an elemental rain and damp pervading everything. Catherine Hardwicke began *Twilight* with a trip to Forks with Jamie Marshall, the first assistant director; Andi Isaacs, a Summit senior vice president of production; and Gillian Bohrer, a Summit creative executive. They also visited the surrounding forests, La Push Beach on the Quileute Indian reservation, and the town of Port Angeles. "We went to the exact places in the book and took photographs and absorbed the atmosphere. Forks has a real sense of community, everybody knows everybody. There are families that go back a hundred years. A local chamber of commerce person named Diane Shostack was our guide in Forks and Port Angeles, and her family has been in logging and forestry and has lived there a hundred years. As you might imagine, everyone in Forks was excited by *Twilight*, which brings in visitors every week."

Two months after Hardwicke's visit, supervising location manager James Lin scouted the area. On the drive in he noticed areas where mass logging had clear-cut forests, a stark contrast when they arrived at dense native growth with green moss growing untouched for hundreds of years. On the Quileute reservation, he saw young people who were a blend of hip-hop culture and Native pride. On La Push Beach he checked out catch pools and tidal basins and pieces of driftwood hundreds of feet long that had been there for decades, worn smooth to the touch by the surf. Along the way, Lin made notes in a journal and shot panoramic photographic views with his Nikon digital camera or his good old-fashioned Nikon .35 millimeter. "I give the director the closest representation of what exists," explained Lin. "Catherine likes to use different elements and the scouting [report] helps jog her memory, maybe even inspire her to try something different."

Scouting begins by taking "the lay of the land," Lin explains, which means talking to locals, including the chamber of commerce and any film commission serving the location of interest. That research serves as a springboard for "hitting the pavement," as Lin puts it, driving around and keeping one's eyes open. Instinct guides a scout, along with a little luck. It was while scouting in Kentucky for *The Insider* that Lin met his wife, but his next

Rob Pattinson and Kristen Stewart on the set of Forks High School

all-time find was on *Into the Blue*, a feature filming in the Bahamas. He had been asked to find a water tank for simulating swimming in open water, but none were readily available. It seemed an impossible task. One day, while driving along the ocean, he spotted an open field and, behind thick overgrowth, what looked like five gigantic oil tanks. He threw a rock at one— it made the echoing sound of an empty tank. In reality, he had discovered molasses storage tanks used by the Bacardi Rum company. Lin met the head of the company, Juan Bacardi himself, an expatriate from Cuba in his seventies who loved America and agreed to let the filmmakers use the tank. It had been drained for cleaning and was 32 feet deep, 125 feet wide, and held 1.2 million gallons of molasses. The production painted it blue, spent a few days pumping in a million gallons of ocean water, and had their

controllable environment for simulating open ocean—all because of a chance sighting and one fortuitously thrown rock.

"You're always looking for interesting things," Lin reflected. "It might be a place you find by chance at the right time of day, maybe a place at sunset where the light is a certain way and sells the location. The great thing about Catherine on this show was even if it wasn't in the script, she wanted to put anything into the movie that said Pacific Northwest—the land, lifestyle, any great architecture. That's great when someone is flexible enough to integrate things people typically don't see."

Lin's two months of preproduction prep work scouted places that would be photographically interesting and serve the story. The production staff, led by the director, production designer, and cinematographer, could then evaluate locations as to whether they could work for story needs and the logistics of filming. "I'm responsible for whether a location is shootable," noted director of photography Elliot Davis. "I always feel things will reveal themselves—in film, or in life, they always do. We consider what we can do, whether we can take advantage of a location. What are the logistics—can I get cameras and cranes and lighting equipment there? The criteria is how to stage our actors. Catherine might also have a specific idea and, because she's a visual person, an image might be building in her mind of how to do [a certain scene], and her concerns are whether a particular location will do that. If a location doesn't work, we have to keep looking."

Forks and its environs *were* the story, and had the requisite beautiful locations, but lacked the housing and infrastructure necessary for a film crew on a tight budget. With a bigger budget "you would just make it happen," Davis noted, but the "budget crunch" doomed Hardwicke's desire to follow in the footsteps of the novel. The production team, determined to be faithful to the book, had to find a substitute for Forks.

> FORKS AND ITS ENVIRONS *were* THE STORY, AND HAD THE REQUISITE BEAUTIFUL LOCATIONS, BUT LACKED THE HOUSING AND INFRASTRUCTURE NECESSARY FOR A FILM CREW ON A TIGHT BUDGET.

St. Helens, OR, was also used as the location of Port Angeles, WA.

33

own the rugged coastline from the events of *Twilight*, the production recreated the world in physical locations. The stand-in for Forks would be a composite of places in and around Portland, Oregon, including Vernonia and St. Helens.

Lin and his key assistant location managers Beth Melnick and Don Baldwin undertook a new scout of the Portland area. The scouting team included an additional scout in Portland and two assistant location managers from Los Angeles for when second unit filming began and additional staff would be needed to make sure upcoming locations had the requisite permissions and were prepped for filming. As much as possible, the new locations would match locales already scouted in the Forks area. "Our scouts would say when something wasn't right," producer Godfrey noted. "It was that extra level of effort and work that went into capturing the world of *Twilight*. Our first priority was to nail the book, and Portland was a good match for Forks. It's in the Pacific Northwest, you're only a couple hundred miles away [from Forks], and there's a gloominess to the weather."

The weather. In that respect, the Portland area proved too good a match to that wettest town in the continental USA. Informational packets provided to production members ahead of principal photography warned they were headed for rain country and to come prepared. Hardwicke, for one, visited a wilderness supply store and posed the question: "What can I wear so that I can stand out in the freezing rain for

Outside the Columbia Theatre, St. Helens, OR

fourteen hours a day and not get wet?" She came away with a hat, jackets and rain pants, a neck warmer, long underwear, wool socks of every thickness, and Gore-Tex boots, all *guaranteed* to keep her warm and dry. But, as James Lin notes, when one stands out in rain all day, *there is no protection.*

In seeking to emulate the cloudy, rainy atmosphere of Forks, the production staff thought it had found a reasonable substitute in Oregon, notes art director Ian Phillips. "We went to the Portland area because you'll have rain and damp, but not severe weather and complete downpours [as in Forks]. But, as I understand it, when we went there to film, Portland was having one of its worst winters in quite some time. It wasn't supposed to be that wet, it just ended up that way."

Some crew members admitted it was one thing to anticipate harsh weather and prepare for it, another to experience and endure it. They faced the very reality Bella Swan observed when she arrived from Arizona to Washington: "When I landed in Port Angeles, it was raining. I didn't see it as an omen—just unavoidable. I'd already said my goodbyes to the sun."[9]

"The rain was horrifying, you have no idea!" makeup department head Jeanne Van Phue groaned in recollection. "It's really hard to put makeup on wet skin when your brushes are wet. I knew it was going to be wet, but I'd never been to Portland and I didn't think it would be *as* wet. There were only four days, the entire time we were shooting, when it didn't rain. After the first day of shooting, everyone was soaking wet, like drowned rats. But our wonder-

BELLA SWAN OBSERVED WHEN SHE ARRIVED FROM ARIZONA TO WASHINGTON: "WHEN I LANDED IN PORT ANGELES, IT WAS RAINING. I DIDN'T SEE IT AS AN OMEN— JUST UNAVOIDABLE. I'D ALREADY SAID MY GOODBYES TO THE SUN."

ful producers, Wyck Godfrey and Michele Imperato Stabile, were so great—they got us tents with heaters that first week, plus they had makeup lights and mirrors for us on location, and a warming tent for the actors so they could be comfortable when lights were being set up. Steve Smith, our amazing key grip, also put up a twenty-by-twenty-foot butterfly on the camera crane, a tarp which bounces light, but which also covered our actors. But even then, there was mist and the wind would blow rain onto you."

"It was tough; we had to have blow dryers and curling irons and dry towels ready all the time," hair stylist Mary Ann Valdes added. "We had to shield the actors from the rain, keep umbrellas over them, because when hair gets wet it'll take a half hour to get them ready to come back again. If they lose time, they get behind in the schedule, and that gets into money."

The main problem was not rain alone, but the mercurial nature of the weather, Godfrey added. "As much as it was likely to rain every day, you could also get hail and snow and sun. It was a crisis of how to match our locations with each scene, and keep our movie on time, when the weather kept changing." The bottom line

was shifting weather conditions combined with "a very aggressive schedule," Godfrey added. Each day of the tight shooting schedule was a day that couldn't be wasted, and they also had special time restrictions for actors under eighteen, in particular Kristen Stewart, who was in nearly every scene and a minor until two and a half weeks before the end of shooting. "For her birthday she got a big cake with a clock!" Hardwicke recalled. "And then we went directly into night shooting. Welcome to adulthood!"

"Nothing ever goes as planned in the making of a movie, particularly when dealing with complicated shooting schedules and exterior shooting conditions, and winters in Portland," set decorator Gene Serdena observed. "The level of craftsmanship on movies [means] everyone is a professional, and you try to be as meticulous and organized as you can be—and

then a big cosmic wrench gets thrown into the works and everyone is constantly scrambling to find a way to pull this thing off. It's a miracle any movie gets made!"

Throughout filming there was often a reminder of what was at stake in translating the publishing phenomenon to the big screen—young *Twilight* fans, many having traveled hundreds of miles, standing for hours through rain and deep into cold nights, watching from the perimeters of various location shoots. The "Twilighters" were rewarded with visits by Hardwicke, Pattinson, Stewart, and others who signed autographs and chatted with the happy fans. "They would hang out for hours in the cold and wet, waiting for Rob and Kristen and everyone to come out," Van Phue recalled. "I don't think [the actual filmmaking] even mattered to them. I was amazed."

"FOR HER BIRTHDAY SHE GOT A BIG CAKE WITH A CLOCK!" HARDWICKE RECALLED. "AND THEN WE WENT DIRECTLY INTO NIGHT SHOOTING. WELCOME TO ADULTHOOD!"

Hardwicke discussing a shot with DP Elliot Davis

*T*wilight, as with most productions, was shot out of sequence, its schedule determined by the vagaries of weather, availability of sets and locations, and other factors. For example, due to an actor's availability, principal photography began with the finale, the dramatic battle for Bella's life between Edward and a murderous vampire in a dance studio, which was filmed on a soundstage set built in Portland. But the production and first assistant director, Jamie Marshall, always had to be ready to shoot as the weather dictated. The latter point was of particular concern to director of photography Elliot Davis and his lighting and camera crew.

"The challenge of the movie was like the Chinese saying: 'Bad foundation, whole house fall down,'" Davis said. "The foundation was I couldn't allow sunlight to penetrate the vampires' world; we had to keep a cloudy look at all times. Sunlight is what makes them turn with what we called the 'sparkle effect,' which we were saving for one of the climaxes of the movie when Edward reveals himself to Bella. The Cullen kids don't even come to school when it's sunny, claiming their parents take them on field trips. It was a big stated law in this movie. Even if they could be in shade, we couldn't see sunlight in the background. I never watched weather reports like I did on this movie! At night, before I went to sleep, I'd check out the five-day forecast. I felt like a weather forecaster! My hierarchy of preference was clouds, drizzle,

"AT NIGHT, BEFORE I WENT TO SLEEP, I'D CHECK OUT THE FIVE-DAY FORECAST. I FELT LIKE A WEATHER FORECASTER! MY HIERARCHY OF PREFERENCE WAS CLOUDS, DRIZZLE, RAIN, THEN SLEET AND SNOW. ALL WERE BETTER THAN SUN."

rain, then sleet and snow. All were better than sun. Sometimes you had to have the patience to wait [for clouds], which is very hard when you're under pressure and spending money, where every second is a dollar and you're watching your day go."

Davis, like Hardwicke, was a trained architect—"that's one of our bonds, I guess," he says with a smile. Davis gravitated to filmmaking with a thesis film on urban recycling systems. A subsequent film about kids who escape a mental institution made the film festival rounds, and he enrolled at UCLA film school. His first film job was with the late Jacques Cousteau, the famed explorer of the sea.

Davis felt it was a natural transition from architecture to movies. "Film is a very architectural medium. Film has a long history of architecture, from German Expressionism and Fritz Lang's *Metropolis*, to the looks of film *noir*, which is very graphic in the way it treats light, shadow, and space. Locations and buildings and what rooms and spaces are going to look like are as much a part of films as the actors. I see a place in terms of light and space—it becomes a character in the movie. And we have to think about what happens in that space. Like all architectural people, I'm a believer in form follows function. The director is free to imagine something, it falls to the rest of us how to do that! For the camera work there are dollies and tracks, but all those are just ways to get cameras from Point A to Point B, to follow the action."

The camera work emphasized a handheld approach, a documentary style with cameras moving in and around actors. One of the cinematographic tools was the Steadicam

"LOCATIONS AND BUILDINGS AND WHAT ROOMS AND SPACES ARE GOING TO LOOK LIKE ARE AS MUCH A PART OF FILMS AS THE ACTORS."

camera operated by George Billinger. "We used a lot of Steadicam, more than we used dollies, because we wanted the feeling the camera could go places and not be restricted," Davis explained. "The Steadicam is basically a camera on a flexible arm that is harnessed around the body of the operator, and the arm that holds the camera goes off the harness. It's stabilized on gyros that allow the camera to move; it takes out all the vibrations and keeps the horizon stable, so the operator can run with it and the camera won't bounce up and down. We did a lot of handheld so the film would breathe. Many traditional Hollywood films seem formal and we didn't want it to look like actors were in a static box. That sense of life is one advantage documentary films have over dramatic features, and that's the history of Catherine's films; she likes the *cinéma vérité* look."

The production planned out complex scenes, including a vampire baseball game and a fight in the dance studio, for which they shot rehearsals and edited together a "mini-movie," Hardwicke noted. "I storyboarded or photo-boarded all the action. Everything was planned, but often the weather or other factors forced us to skip shots and improvise others. Elliot Davis and I tried to find a way to shoot each scene to convey its feeling and emotions. Sometimes the camera was static, but more often it was moving, enhancing the emotional dynamic."

Left to right: Jessica Stanley (Anna Kendrick), Mike Newton (Michael Welch), Bella Swan (Kristen Stewart), and Eric Yorkie (Justin Chon) around the lunch table in the cafeteria

"There's a freedom of movement in actors and cameras because this is a story about a girl breaking into a new place, leaving something behind. Bella is in motion; she's physically on the move from one world to another. That's her journey, from where she thought she was to a place she never thought she could possibly be. All these instruments [of filmmaking] give that feeling to the film, the feeling of moving forward."

—ELLIOT DAVIS

Before the director could direct her actors and the camera crew could film them, the performers had to be in costume with their hair styled and makeup applied. "Wardrobe, hair, makeup—it all has to look unified or it's not going to work," hair stylist Mary Ann Valdes explained. "Our three departments work closely together. Wardrobe usually leads the process, because hair and makeup is a little more flexible, while costumes have to be decided ahead of time and things have to be fitted. The kind of clothes being worn will also accentuate the makeup."

For costume designer Wendy Chuck, whose credits include *Sideways*, the accelerated timetable of modern movie making is far from the days when the luxury of months of preproduction were the rule, not the exception. "Now you get a script, you get the actors, and we go shopping," Chuck said. "Things happen fast and furious. I have a budget, so in addition to the creative element and supporting the actors, there are economic concerns. There's a lot to consider."

The *Twilight* costume department included seven crew members in Los Angeles, and twelve to fifteen in Portland to handle everything needed for Hardwicke's first unit and Andy Cheng's second unit, with outside manufacturers hired to produce made-to-order costumes. "Every show is different, but costume design for this show was a combination of buying off the rack and having things made," Chuck explained.

Even when clothing was bought off the rack, it had to be aged to look lived-in and realistic. Chuck was aided by Janet Cadmus, who worked with the Portland opera company and was expert at aging costumes to fit the life of a character. Costumes often were prepared in multiples to serve specific purposes, such as stunts that required outfits to be specially prepared to hide harnesses and provide pick points for flying wire work. Much of the work was set in motion, Chuck notes, before the crew left for Portland, with fittings in Los Angeles often determining special costumes. The character of James (played by Cam Gigandet), one of the nomadic vampires who hunts Bella, needed a longer leather jacket that wouldn't hike up when he had to raise his arms overhead as he was being flown for wire work. That special jacket was manufactured in Hollywood and became one of the stream of special costume orders shipped to Portland throughout principal photography.

The costumes had to reflect the story and the nature of each character, becoming an organic process as actors began bringing their characters to life. "To me there were three worlds: Bella's world, which includes Forks High School, the Cullen family world, and the Native American world we see at La Push Beach and with the character of [Quileute elder] Billy Black and his son, Jacob," Chuck observed. "I start with a big palette and, as the weeks go by, things become more refined as the actors and all of us make choices.

Actor Taylor Lautner displays Jacob Black's infectious charm.

> "THE GENERAL MOOD WAS THIS IS A LOVE STORY COUNTERPOINTED BY THE ADVENTURE STORY."

The charge was to keep as close to the book as possible, and we were all driven to support the overall look. The general mood was this is a love story counterpointed by the adventure story. The bones were already there; it was a matter of fleshing them out and bringing them alive. There were clues in the book and the screenplay on how characters would be dressed.

Although Bella generally wears regular or corduroy jeans (an exception is the dress she wears for the high school prom at film's end), Kristen Stewart's outfits reflected Isabella Swan's

"WHEN SHE FALLS IN LOVE WITH EDWARD, AND MERGES WITH THE CULLEN WORLD, HER PALETTE GOES TO MORE COOL COLORS; HER CLOTHES BECOME A LITTLE SOFTER AND ROMANTIC, LESS TOMBOY."

transformation as the story unfolded. "Bella starts as a tomboy, with warm, earthy colors," Chuck explained. "She's from the Southwest and her mother is a bit of a hippie, so she reflects that, with eclectic looks and funky bits of jewelry—palette-wise she doesn't fit in with the other high school kids. She's arrived from Arizona with only a few things, so she's not dressed appropriately for the weather in Forks. It's cold and damp, a different world from what she knows. A little backstory is she finds a jacket at her dad's house, some old vintage coat. When she falls in love with Edward, and merges with the Cullen world, her palette goes to more cool colors; her clothes become a little softer and romantic, less tomboy."

The hair design for Stewart also reflected different points in the story. "I begin with a script and do a breakdown and ask questions about what's needed for each sequence," hair department head Mary Ann Valdes added. "The movie is shot out of sequence, so we also have to match everything. You might shoot an indoors scene and then, three weeks later, they'll shoot exteriors of the same scene, so my staff and I take notes and photographs; we maintain a continuity book. We also had to have the same hairstyles and wigs for doubles."

For Bella, Valdes had first gone online to check out pictures of the actress, to get a feel for what her hair was like. When Stewart arrived for *Twilight*, her hair was colored light red with black streaks from a previous film, so the first step was to go to a colorist to make it a "rich, warm brown," which was how Valdes described Bella's hair color. The hair design was determined by production concerns that because

Stewart was still a minor, and had a maximum allowable hours to work each day, the longer she was having her hair done, the less time in front of the camera. "For Kristen I came up with a 'three quarter wig,'" Valdes explained. "We could use her natural part and the front part of her own hair, with the wig fitting like a horseshoe shape around the top of her head and back of the front hair line [and falling in the back]. I could press the wig at night, so when Kristen came in the morning all I'd have to do was the front of her hair, which took about fifteen to twenty minutes, as opposed to a half hour to forty-five minutes to blow-dry and curl her own hair. I gave the wig more length and volume because there was concern about it holding up in adverse weather. Victoria Wood made all the wigs on the show; they were all human hair."

Charlie Swan, Bella's dad and police chief of Forks (played by Billy Burke), had to reflect "a very simple Northwestern dad," Wendy Chuck noted. As often happens, the actor made suggestions for outfits that would help his character. Charlie watches sports on TV with Billy Black, so Burke asked if the production could get permission for him to wear merchandising related to Washington state professional sports teams. Clearances were ultimately secured that put Charlie in a Seattle Mariners baseball cap and T-shirt.

The production planned to use a real Forks police uniform for Charlie, which arrived a couple days before fitting and was bright and made of high-tech fabric—it didn't look like the

Charlie Swan (Billy Burke, center), introduces Bella (Stewart) to Billy (Gil Birmingham) and Jacob Black (Taylor Lautner) for the first time.

> "The idea behind production design is to create the look and to evoke emotions and ground the characters where they exist, to evoke their history through the visual aspects of the film. We were fortunate in this movie to be able to have some basis in reality and have the vampires based in real places. We tried to reproduce and re-create places so you'd have the feeling you were in Arizona or Forks, Washington."
>
> —IAN PHILLIPS

uniform of a small-town cop, so Chuck "cheated it" with a traditional dark Navy blue policeman's jacket. The rest of Charlie's ensemble was relatively simple. "I found most of his stuff in thrift stores. The actor told me he thought that when Charlie was off-duty he'd get out of his uniform as much as possible. He's not in stunts, so I only needed one of everything. It was jeans, a plaid flannel shirt over a T-shirt, and he always had practical, comfortable boots."

The look of the film was established by the art department, which sought to bring the director's vision to life. "It began with us speaking with Catherine about a character," art director Ian Phillips explained. "For example, we discussed how Charlie's life had progressed and where he was location-wise, whether he lived in town or outside of town. The location department would then bring in photographs of locations and we'd go and physically scout them. After we found a location [interior], I'd measure it and create a floor plan and lay out the furniture placement for the location set so actors could move fluidly throughout the space. After we did the floor plan, we'd do sketches for the overall feel of the location. That then got passed to the set decorator, which for this production was Gene Serdena, and he would go to find items to dress the set."

The sets, whether pre-existing locations modified to suit the story or built on a sound-stage by the production's construction department, all had to appear inhabited by real people and fit into a designed world that included a visual style and color schemes. "My domain is all the physical elements," Serdena explained. "We start with flooring, furniture, wall covering, lights, fixtures, drapes, and go right down to details like the notes characters pin to bulletin boards, the selection of books on a bookshelf, the things in a drawer. The visual concept and palette have been developed [by the production designer and art department] early on. I just take that and run with it."

"We tried to replicate and contrast the vibrancy of Arizona with Washington," Phillips added. "Washington is lush, green and vivid, and we knew Forks was a small town, so we wanted it very simply styled, with a lot of older buildings and a main street, small and quaint, a place vampires could hide without people knowing. We wanted a small-town feel that fit the frame of the camera—the real town of Forks actually has a wide main street."

The Forks of the film was shot in Vernonia, Oregon. The interior and exterior of Bella's house was shot in St. Helens, which was also used as the Port Angeles locations: the interior dress shop, the exterior of the bookstore, and the interior and exterior of the restaurant. "Forks and Vernonia are both in the mountains and surrounded by forests," Phillips said. "St. Helens is kind of in flatlands and we were able to create interiors for a bookstore and dress shop from the book."

The reason Vernonia wasn't used for interiors, Phillips explained, was the town had flooded from a storm and hurricane force winds in November of 2007. An exception was an old bank building that had been high enough to escape flood damage and was used for the police station interior. A two-foot waterline still marked the interiors of buildings when Phillips visited the town. "Vernonia is a logging town, probably late 1800s to early 1900s," Phillips said. "The logging, of course, reflected logging in Washington. St. Helens was also used for our location of Port Angeles, where Edward and Bella have dinner, because Port Angeles is a port town and St. Helens sits on a river. A lot of the Port Angeles scenes take place at night, so we just needed reflections of the water, as opposed to seeing the town. It also had to be a different town to contrast with Vernonia."

Charlie's home, which becomes Bella's home, was one of the major locations that served as both an interior and exterior location set. (Gene Serdena estimates there were fifty to

sixty different location sets. Of that number, probably twenty-five were real places, not fabricated sets, adapted by the art department, paint, construction, and other departments for filming purposes.) Location scouting had initially discovered a house in Carver, a town outside Portland, that seemed perfect for Charlie, a weather-beaten old place with an overgrowth of dead vines on one side and a roof covered in emerald moss. "We fell in love with that house," Phillips recalled. "For Charlie we wanted to create a house that had been a loving home, but then he gets a divorce and has been living by himself for quite some time. He's an older father and has had a family [before the divorce], so it wasn't a typical single man's bachelor pad. He was also a civil servant, so he didn't have a lot of money. The house that was found also satisfied [story concerns] that he live outside of town. But due to some structural problems we were unable to use it."

The production switched to a house originally spotted by Hardwicke on her first scout of St. Helens. It was more conventional-looking, but ended up better serving the character, in Gene Serdena's opinion. "We had certain character notions to develop within the architecture of that space. We wanted to develop the idea with the home that Charlie was a guy buried in his work, a guy who starts projects and doesn't

necessarily pay attention to the condition of his home. I said to Catherine that I thought Charlie would be the type of guy who probably never ate at the dining room table, but at the table where he paid his bills or worked on a carburetor. She liked that idea, and we tried to develop that character within the house throughout all the spaces you might see.

"I think the attraction of the first location was the exterior satisfied a number of conditions intrinsic to the story, such as allowing a character to look out the window and feel Forks was this remote and exotic location," Serdena added. "And the exterior would have been beautiful to photograph. But it was dilapidated and kind of derelict, with a specific atmosphere. There was a level of negligence that might have invited judgment, since we know Charlie is a divorced bachelor. That first house made a statement that insinuated his life was unraveling, like he was a kind of bum. The second house was more conventional, but the physical space altered the way you would view that character. It was interesting that it wound up serving the character better than the previous location would have."

Ultimately, a set is about conveying character. As an example, Serdena cites a desk Charlie buys for Bella's bedroom. A seemingly minor detail, it spoke volumes about Charlie, and from there the heroine's living space evolved

"AS BELLA SETTLED IN AND WE RETURNED TO HER ROOM, CATHERINE WANTED TO HAVE DISTINCT LOOKS OF PROGRESS, AS THOUGH BELLA WAS ADDING MORE PERSONAL TOUCHES."

"I often feel the way I approach my work is similar to the approach an actor takes towards developing a character. It's been a skill I've had to develop over the years. When I was newer to this game, I thought it was about pure design and aesthetically pleasing interiors. As I've grown in my career, my perception and concerns have shifted to be anchored specifically in character. In the beginning stages of a design, I'll have pure discussions and the script is sort of the bible for satisfying the conditions of the story. When I do my first pass of a script, I do a breakdown. The script might say, 'She crosses the room and sits in a chair, turns on a lamp and picks up a telephone.' As a set decorator, you need to get all those things, but you also need other things—and subtext. Some stories offer you a great deal to understand a character. You have to draw on that inner something to figure out what a character is all about. It's absolutely an evolutionary process."

—GENE SERDENA

throughout the story. "Perhaps her father has made a modest attempt to brighten the room with a new desk. So, where do you get a desk when you're the police chief in a remote town in upstate Washington? Charlie would probably go to Seattle and a Staples or an Office Max; it wouldn't be an antique, rolltop desk.

"As Bella settled in and we returned to her room, Catherine wanted to have distinct looks of progress, as though Bella was adding more personal touches," Serdena added. "One touch we added was the notion that when Bella was younger and her parents were still married, she and her mother had worked on arts and crafts projects together. I made a series of flags of colorful tissue paper that toys with the notion that they were too sophisticated to have been made by a child alone, that she made them with her mother. So these arts and crafts items start appearing. It's all subliminal, all backstory."

Bella's bedroom, Serdena added, was one of "those evolving spaces" that posed logistical and continuity challenges. The director of photography had special concerns because Edward would visit Bella there, so there had to be a romantic look to the way light could filter through the room. Bella's room also became a designated "cover set." Typically, a cover set would be built by the construction department,

dismantled, and trucked to a location where it would be assembled, painted, and dressed. But Bella's bedroom would be created and then duplicated directly at one of the other locations. Measurements were first made of the room at the St. Helens location that had been selected to be Bella's room. That set was duplicated at a utility shed at the remote Colombia River Gorge where the production was shooting outdoor footage. Instead of waiting out harsh weather at that location, the crew could switch to shooting interior scenes of Bella's room.

"There was a narrow window for acceptable weather conditions, so we needed these cover sets at the ready—the ultimate goal was not to lose time," Serdena said. "But Bella's bedroom would switch from interior scenes to the exterior shots of her looking out a window at the Charlie house location, then they would come back and revisit the cover set at the Colombia River Gorge. Since they didn't shoot in sequence it was a logistical nightmare to figure things out. There are basically three versions of Bella's bedroom over the course of the film [reflecting the lived-in changes]. What I did was I first dressed Bella's room at the beginning, a middle, and an end. I photographed each one and restored it to the beginning stage where we started shooting."

Set decorator Gene Serdena's department

FORKS IS A STRANGE PLACE TO A GIRL FROM THE PHOENIX METROPOLITAN AREA— WAY TOO WET AND GREEN AND SMALL...

included his regular three-person team from Los Angeles as well as Portland locals who provided invaluable tips on where to get everything from an old piece of hardware to fishing poles. Serdena had also made a preproduction trip to the location to see what set dressing items might be available. He then rented what he thought he might need from Los Angeles prop houses and shipped it all to a Portland warehouse. Although he was far from the controlled environment of a Hollywood soundstage, Serdena welcomed the challenges of working on location. "Most of the time, for me, it's actually more interesting to work on location. A location suggests things; it'll have an attitude. The imperfections you find at a location tend to be more interesting, and harder to achieve, for stage sets. It's almost impossible, for example, to make up the look of old curtains that don't hang too well but have been hanging in a home for thirty years, [and

the other] design solutions people come up with in their own homes."

In the novel, Forks is a strange place to a girl from the Phoenix metropolitan area—way too wet and green and small, far from the valley heat and urban sprawl she left behind. She gets a pair of wheels by way of Charlie's friend Billy, but it's as funky as the weather. "Bella's truck had to look like it had been out in rain and rough weather," said Ian Phillips, whose work included coming up with the right automobiles for the characters. "We started with a brand-new paint job, and our paint department refinished it to look rusted, like an older, worn truck."

Even from afar, the town supported the filmmakers. For the high school, the principal of Forks High School provided the production with examples of school graphics, banners, and yearbooks. The movie version of the school was made up of different locations that had to be seamlessly filmed and edited together for the illusion of a single place. "It's all about finding spaces that allow you to photograph something and allow you to create the specific atmosphere you want to develop," Serdena noted. "Fortunately, the diligent work of the location manager came up with a composite school. That's filmmaking, to take several separate schools composited together to make the fictional Forks High School."

The high school Hardwicke visited in Forks actually had a big, modern new wing attached to the old school, which was a little brick building. The production went old school when they tried to match the real Forks H.S. "We found a brick building that looked like the old part of Forks High about a three or four hour drive from Forks at Kalama High School in Kalama, Washington," Hardwicke recalled. "We also shot at Madison High School in Portland because it was easier to film there; there were windows to put lights and do other practical things."

Bella's arrival at the high school now made the student body 358, not in the same league as her former high school with its enrollment of 3,000 students. The students at Forks all know each other in that small-town way, and Bella

"It isn't Manhattan or Beverly Hills, but the kids in Forks are not from Podunk, either—it's more generic USA. The phenomenon of the Internet has changed these smaller towns. Kids buy off the Internet, although their clothes are appropriate for the weather. The thing that surprised me [in Oregon] was they wear hoodies and jeans, but they hardly ever wear raincoats! They just get damp and go indoors. That struck me as a little different. I wouldn't have gotten that from the research. We would have our extras come in and they didn't have raincoats. I didn't ask them, but I assume it just wasn't considered cool. It looked a little wrong. I had to give a little more flavor to their clothing than I wanted."

—WENDY CHUCK

Jasper Hale (Jackson Rathbone) looks on as Bella (Stewart) speaks to Alice Cullen (Ashley Greene) and Edward (Pattinson).

"What drove all the visual imagery was Bella and Edward's relationship. In the school we tried to shoot very intimately. It was about how they look at each other, how they notice each other. We had very tight shots, roaming over bodies. It was like, when you see someone and get attracted to them, what is it that you notice? Is it their eyes, the hair on the back of their neck, their delicate fingers, the shape of their mouth? The first impression is what we tried to hit."

—ELLIOT DAVIS

Costume Designer Wendy Chuck (right) and Catherine Hardwicke (center) dress Ashley (Alice).

feels like an outsider, but she quickly makes friends, even catching the eye of some of her male classmates. It's at lunchtime that she first sees the Cullens, sitting silently by themselves at the far end of the cafeteria with their trays of untouched food. She learns their names: Jasper and Rosalie Hale, Edward, Emmett, and Alice Cullen, the adopted children of Dr. Carlisle Cullen and his wife Esme. But Bella is strangely drawn to seventeen-year-old Edward.

Edward and Bella find themselves partners in biology class. Gene Serdena credits the head of the biology department at the University of Oregon at Portland (UOP) with helping create a look appropriate to a small-town high school curriculum. The biology classroom set was created at a journalism classroom at Portland's Madison High School and dressed out with items selected from an archival room at UOP that included reconstructed skeletons, a twisted branch holding a dried wasp's nest, a stuffed owl, decomposed animals, and amphibious creatures suspended in gelatinous liquids. The classroom had the look of a rural high school, right down to lab tables with old-fashioned slate tops made by the production staff. "We tried not to push the apparatus in the classroom to be too state-of-the-art," Serdena noted. "There's no bubbling chemistry experiment in the background; we kept it very organic-looking. I also went to Catherine and said there had to be a certain romantic quality to this classroom, that we should incorporate a picturesque something, like flowers, because the biology class is where Edward and Bella fall in love."

BELLA IS STRANGELY DRAWN TO SEVENTEEN-YEAR-OLD EDWARD.

Elliot Davis (DP, center) with Kristen and Rob on the set of the biology classroom

Secrets of the Vampires

Carlisle (Facinelli) at Edward's (Pattison) deathbed during the flu epidemic, in another flashback scene

Bella realizes there is something strangely different about Edward and the Cullens and tries to find out their secret. "In *Twilight*, Bella tries to figure out exactly who or what Edward is," Hardwicke explained. "In one sequence, we show illustrations and descriptions of some of the more obscure vampire legends. She researches the various vampire myths and realizes the descriptions synch up with what she knows about Edward, unraveling the mystery."

Edward finally shows Bella his vampire side during what the production called "the reveal," the scene that is the soul of *Twilight*, the scene that Stephenie Meyer dreamed, that intense conversation between a girl and a vampire in a meadow. It is there that Edward exults in his seductive, predatory power to lure this potential victim to a deserted place where she's powerless to stop him from taking her. "He says, 'I never wanted to kill a human being as much as you!'" Hardwicke noted. "That's the heart of it. She loves him and he's a killer. Edward has so much inner conflict and turmoil and angst—he doesn't want to be a monster. And then, out of this utter despair, he falls in love with his soul mate and begins to see hope and light and a chance that life could be better. Stephenie built so many contradictions into this character, and that's what attracted Robert Pattinson to this role."

In Meyer's story, Edward Cullen was born in Chicago in 1901. He was seventeen when he took ill and was taken to a hospital, about to become another statistic of the Spanish influenza epidemic. A vampire doctor named Carlisle Cullen saved him by making him one of his own—the first of others he would similarly save. Pattinson also did his own exploratory work to

Meet the Cullens' other children: (left to right) Emmet Cullen (Kellan Lutz), Rosalie Hale (Nikki Reed), Alice Cullen (Greene), and Jasper Hale (Rathbone) in the hallways of Forks High.

In a flashback scene, Dr. Carlisle Cullen (Peter Facinelli) changes his future wife Esme (Elizabeth Reaser), saving her from certain death.

get into Edward's head, including, the director recalls, writing pained letters to his vampire father asking, "Why did you convert me—*why did you change me?*"

"Rob Pattinson did so much personal work to create a character who has been emotionally dead for a hundred years but is reawakened by Bella," Wyck Godfrey recalled. "He created a whole life for this character that went above and beyond the call of duty. You had to be sensitive around him, because it was kind of a dark and sad place to be. Catherine and everyone gave [Pattinson and Stewart] space to do these very intimate scenes. There was the pain and addictive quality of him basically wanting to just reach over and kill Bella, an impulse he's fighting every moment he's with her. Rob played the character as being tortured, which is really the metaphor for young love—it hurts, it's great, it's maddening. He brought that element to it. He becomes obsessed with her, the same way she is with him."

The production's verisimilitude included a realistic approach to vampires. "These vampires don't have fangs, or turn into bats—you have vampires walking around high school, which in and of itself is part of the charm of the book," Godfrey added. "Stephenie Meyer made you feel these things were real, and we had to make sure we got that right, that we had the right methodology to show supernatural elements in a way that felt real. If it was wire work, we had to make sure the actors [and stunt doubles] didn't look like they were hanging on wires. It had to be believable and fluid. We don't have faces transforming into demonic looks; we didn't film actors on a greenscreen stage and create environments behind them. We had organic settings and went old school; we actually had people jumping out of trees and flying through glass walls. That was a very deliberate choice."

In December of 2007, three months before *Twilight* principal photography, Richard Kidd's visual effects team, Andy Cheng's stunt team, and Andy Weder's special effects unit convened in a forested area outside Los Angeles to test cameras, rigs, and setups to determine which effects could be done physically (or "in-camera") and which might need to be augmented with postproduction digital work. The R&D included tests for possible cameras and rigs for a major sequence dubbed the "vampire baseball game." For slow-motion effects for the baseball game, tests were made with a high-speed HD digital camera capable of shooting up to 1,000 frames per second (f.p.s.), Kidd noted. (In motion picture photography, the higher the frame rate over the normal 24 frames per second—the rate found to best convey live action and motion blur—the slower it appears when projected at normal speed.) "We didn't use digital cameras when the real shooting began, but that preproduction work allowed us to develop the slo-mo shots we wanted for practical techniques," Kidd added.

The fruits of the slo-mo research included a camera rig dubbed the "Crazy Horse Rig," named after a movie in which it had been used. "The Crazy Horse was basically two regular film cameras rigged to be off-set, one on top of the other," Kidd explained. "They would shoot through a mirror with a beam splitter, so as the light comes straight through to one camera it gets reflected down with the mirror and back up to the second camera. This would allow us to take two pictures, at nearly the same angle, of the exact same action. The advantage was we could shoot with one camera at 24 frames per second, and the other we could shoot at 144 f.p.s. for slow-motion effects. Then, in postproduction editing, we could seamlessly cut

"WE HAD ORGANIC SETTINGS AND WENT OLD SCHOOL; WE ACTUALLY HAD PEOPLE JUMPING OUT OF TREES AND FLYING THROUGH GLASS WALLS. THAT WAS A VERY DELIBERATE CHOICE."

Hardwicke directs Pattinson during the final confrontation scenes inside the dance studio.

Emmet (Lutz), Alice (Greene), and Jasper (Rathbone)
leap into the fray inside the dance studio set.

"Vampires don't fly, but they can jump and run faster than a human. So eight guys rig up these counterweight balance systems, and you do a cable on a person and have them run or be pulled in harnesses. Andy Cheng is fantastic and fun and created all the cool stunts. He was Jackie Chan's stunt double for ten years—he was in the *Rush Hour* movies, and had all these creative ideas. The vampires are not martial artists, but we were able to adapt some of those techniques they use on these beautiful [Hong Kong] movies to make them work for us."

—CATHERINE HARDWICKE

from regular speed to slow motion of the same shot."

When computer generated imagery was used, it would not be to create a CG stunt figure or a wholly virtual world, but to subtly enhance action and environments. The reality-based approach was also a response to a growing audience interest in seeing action unadorned with CG effects. "I think you feel it; when it's in-camera, you get a dose of visceral energy," Godfrey said. "There's always going to be the crazy, high-concept supernatural movies where reality is bent, like *The Matrix* and *Wanted*. But if the premise of the movie is to make audiences feel these things are real, you're better off shooting with a real methodology, rather than creating artifice."

Godfrey cited the *Bourne* series, wherein Matt Damon plays an assassin trained to be a virtual killing machine who becomes an amnesic, as an example of a crowd-pleasing movie that didn't need to be muscled up with CG enhancement. Damon himself stars in fighting scenes, and explosions and car crashes and other stunts happen in front of the camera. The *Bourne* precedent was also mentioned by stunt coordinator and second unit director Andy Cheng, whose filmmaking roots were in a world of hard-boiled action that had always been doing it "for real." In *Twilight*, Cheng was bringing Hong Kong style to the vampire world.

In "Hong Kong style," elaborate fight scenes feature the star actor, who usually stands

> "I THINK YOU FEEL IT; WHEN IT'S IN-CAMERA, YOU GET A DOSE OF VISCERAL ENERGY."

down only for a stuntman to step in for the "reaction" payoff which requires dangerous stunt work. Andy Cheng felt a breakthrough adaptation of Hong Kong style was *The Matrix*, which featured kung-fu action and had star Keanu Reeves doing a lot of fighting himself (although that film included considerable CG stunts and effects). The success of *Matrix* changed perceptions in the American film business and was his ticket to Hollywood, Cheng feels.

"I moved to America seven years ago and I came with a lot of ideas of how to combine Hong Kong style and Hollywood style," Cheng recalled. "The difference is in Hong Kong movies there's [martial arts] fighting and a fight scene can go on for twenty minutes! In Hollywood it's what we call 'cowboy style,' where it's like one punch, maybe then they break a chair over someone—basically, a punch and then a stunt, with not a lot of choreography. But in the last five years it's changed [in America] to where you see Matt Damon in *The Bourne Identity* doing long choreographed fighting in one take."

Cheng's path to Hollywood began when he was twelve and growing up in Hong Kong. He had gone to see *Police Story*, the 1985 action thriller directed by and starring Jackie Chan as a maverick H.K. cop. A stunt gone awry was in the final film—a hijacked double-decker bus violently brakes in front of Chan's character and a one-car blockade, sending three stunt men crashing though the bus windows but missing the car that would have cushioned their fall, hitting asphalt instead. Not only did the scene inspire an awestruck Cheng to become a stunt-man, he was thrilled to recognize the scene had been staged in his own neighborhood. Cheng would not only eventually serve as stunt double for his cinematic hero, Jackie Chan, but Chan would take him to America to work with him on the *Rush Hour* movies.

Andy Cheng's dream of becoming a stuntman in Hong Kong cinema meant learning martial arts, and he began with classic Chinese forms patterned after the movements of a crane and tiger. Chinese kung-fu emphasizes solo forms, so

> HARDWICKE AND CHENG BOTH AGREED *Twilight* VAMPIRES WOULD BE MORE POWERFUL THAN HUMANS, BUT NOT SUPER-POWERFUL, LIKE THE X-MEN OR SPIDER-MAN.

for organized sparring he took up the Korean art of Tae Kwon Do. From 1987 to 1992, Cheng recalls, he reigned as Tae Kwon Do champion in Hong Kong Black Belt Competition and, in 1991, won a bronze medal at the Asian Games. Around 1989, while still training in competitive fighting, he applied for the stunt class at TVB, one of the Hong Kong television stations that always needed stunt-men under contract for the action fare that was the staple of H.K. television programming. His arduous stunt training included tumbling and trampoline, wire work, weapons, reactions, and a variety of martial arts styles. "You get more

Hardwicke works through the fight scenes with Kristen.

skill, you get more work," Cheng recalled. Back then, he was "a training machine," by day training to be a stuntman, by night preparing for martial arts competitions. Being five feet seven inches tall, with a top weight of 140 pounds, he reduced himself to 116 pounds to make a lower weight category for Tae Kwon Do competition through training and a daily diet of six crackers divided across three meals.

For *Twilight*, Cheng and his fourteen-to-sixteen person team (including eight riggers led by Kevin Chase) came up with wire work for vampire stunts. But at the outset he and the director had to determine "what kind of super-

powers they have," Cheng said. "When I interviewed with Catherine, I said we had to set up what a vampire could do and not do, how fast they could run and how high they could jump."

Cheng's concern was they had to be consistent, that once parameters of a vampire's powers were established they couldn't cheat and deviate. Hardwicke and Cheng both agreed *Twilight* vampires would be more powerful than humans, but not super-powerful, like the X-Men or Spider-Man. Vampires wouldn't fly, but they would have extraordinary jumping abilities. The basic formula for a jump was

Hardwicke and crew direct Rob through a scene in the trees.

twenty feet, with a vampire's form resembling an Olympic long-jumper's propulsion, rise, and descending curve.

"It's a controlled movement, the way a gymnast moves," Hardwicke noted. "Their arms are not flaying, they're in control of their bodies. When vampires run, it's five times [human] speed; they jump and run like a super athlete. There was also a feeling for how vampires move, how much of their animal instincts should come through and how to show that. We studied videos of mountain lions and cougars and different predatory animals in their hunting

mode. We had a choreographer in Portland named Dee Dee Anderson, who works with the Portland Trailblazers basketball team, who taught our 'Cat Class,' with everyone going into crouches. You won't see a lot of this; it was just a subtle thing that informed the movements."

"IF THE PREMISE OF THE MOVIE IS TO MAKE AUDIENCES FEEL THESE THINGS ARE REAL, YOU'RE BETTER OFF SHOOTING WITH A REAL METHODOLOGY, RATHER THAN CREATING ARTIFICE."

THE BASIC FORMULA FOR A JUMP WAS TWENTY
FEET, WITH A VAMPIRE'S FORM RESEMBLING
AN OLYMPIC LONG-JUMPER'S PROPULSION,
RISE, AND DESCENDING CURVE.

*Rob and Kristen
enjoying the wire
work scenes*

"THERE WAS ALSO A FEELING FOR HOW VAMPIRES MOVE, HOW MUCH OF THEIR ANIMAL INSTINCTS SHOULD COME THROUGH AND HOW TO SHOW THAT."

"WE STUDIED VIDEOS OF MOUNTAIN LIONS AND COUGARS AND DIFFERENT PREDATORY ANIMALS IN THEIR HUNTING MODE."

Andy Weder's special effects department included shop foreman Michael Kay, Chris Brenczewski, and Lawrence Decker sharing first unit foreman duties, with key tech Jeff Elliot and Tyan Bardon and Dean Roberts rounding out the tech side. Some of the physical illusions they produced were simplicity itself—for a scene where Bella slips on ice, an "ice wax" material was heated up to 150 degrees in a regular frying pan to create a material that looked like ice but was actually a brittle wax. Ironically, given Mother Nature's regular contributions, the special effects unit sometimes supplied rain effects to a set to match continuity, usually a "wet down" hosing, and several times used rain heads on twelve-foot aluminum poles to sprinkle a rain effect on actors from off-camera.

Special effects also provided atmosphere throughout the film. "It's supposed to be Washington, so we used smoke to give a hazy and smoky atmosphere, or mist, to make things creepier," Weder explained. "We used a technique invented by the English about fifteen years ago. It's called a 'Lay-flat' tube, a six-hundred-foot long inflated tube that's a foot in diameter, with holes in it and a fan with a

smoke machine behind it blowing smoke. I use regular water-based stage smoke. We smoked up a whole mountain! The scene where Edward reveals himself to Bella, we surrounded him with smoke. It's easy to smoke things up on a soundstage, where you can control things, but outdoors, like we were, is always unpredictable. Too much wind can kill you and not enough wind can kill you because the smoke just hangs there."

Weder felt one of his unit's "cool" effects came in the key scene in the Forks High School parking lot in which classmate Tyler Crowley's out-of-control van threatens to ram into Bella and crush her against her own truck. Edward swoops in to her rescue, and with his fantastic physical strength halts the runaway vehicle. It was a risky scene, because the oncoming vehicle would be coming toward the two actors for real.

"The van was on casters, twelve-inch diameter wheels, and on air bags that held the whole thing up about an inch above the ground," Weder explained. "We basically built a steel frame and cut the bottom of the car out and mounted the wheels to that. We had [four guys] pushing it like it was sliding, and we had two 'dead man' ropes on it and attached to

On the rare sunny days, the streets would be hosed down with water to keep continuity.

trucks off-camera. The dead man is basically a limiting cable or rope that will stop something and prevent it from bouncing back. The air bags were like the kind used on the bottom of big trucks, and we had a wire hooked up to the air bag valve so that, with a push of a button, in less than a second the air would go out, the air bags would evacuate, and the whole van dropped down onto its real wheels."

The fail-safe dead man ropes jerked the vehicle to a safe stop, inches from the performers, making it appear the van was stopped by Edward, who holds it off with an outstretched hand and causes the door to buckle. Various materials were tested for a fake door, including a lead door a sixteenth of an inch thick, and a soft aluminum door, which Weder liked. But the director preferred a door made of layers of sheets of industrial-strength aluminum foil built up and attached with spray adhesive. "We formed the aluminum over the real door to get the shape to match perfectly," Weder explained. "Then we flamed out a big hole out of the middle where we wanted the dent to be, and put these sheets on top of that so he could bend and push that section back."

On film, the safety ropes around the van could not, of course, be seen. To seal the illusion, the visual effects department had to remove the telltale ropes. Wire removal is not as sexy as creating full CG environments, but still meat and potatoes in the digital age and allows physical effects and stunt work to produce their seamless physical illusions. Knowing something

"WE FORMED THE ALUMINUM OVER THE REAL
DOOR TO GET THE SHAPE TO MATCH PERFECTLY,"
WEDER EXPLAINED.

"THEN WE FLAMED OUT A BIG HOLE OUT OF THE MIDDLE WHERE WE WANTED THE DENT TO BE, AND PUT THESE SHEETS ON TOP OF THAT SO HE COULD BEND AND PUSH THAT SECTION BACK."

can be digitally removed later has allowed for bigger and safer rigs and setups.

Since *Twilight* was shot on film, the first step for wire removal, and any effects work involving computers, was to digitize the film (once the work was finished, the digital footage could be scanned back out to film). A simple wire removal might need only a "paint-out" technique, with a digital artist painting over the wire or rig using the "information" of the surrounding visual content. Or, if the preceding frame does not have the offending object, a cut and paste technique can use that frame and simply replace the succeeding frame. On *Twilight*, wire removals were needed in unlikely places, such as a scene at the school cafeteria salad bar where Bella accidentally knocks an apple to the floor, but Edward deftly catches it on his shoe and, in a hacky-sack move, pops it up into his hand. The apple was actually connected to a monofilament, the kind used for fishing lines, and manipulated off-camera, but left a thin line running through that had to be digitally removed.

Stronger measures were needed to erase the security ropes used to secure Tyler's runaway van. The van had to be replaced with a completely clean "plate," an old photographic term referring to shots of the backgrounds used in composite photography. On a major visual effects show, a live-action plate for subsequent visual effects composite work is typically prepared just before cameras roll. "In a visual effects shoot, you'd shoot a clean plate by clearing everything out of the frame and popping four to ten seconds of background plate, which gives you the exact angles and height of the shot you have to

replace," Kidd said. The *Twilight* challenge was the director's "fluid and documentary" approach to filming, Kidd added. "We realized Catherine wanted to shoot documentary–style, so we knew each shot wasn't going to be planned out as in a normal visual effects shoot where each effects shot is very designed. Although we knew the script, locations, and rough blocking of the camerawork, we didn't know *exactly* where the camera was going to be. The camera might be coming in five inches off the ground or five feet, and from different angles. To do the cable replacement, still photographs were taken of the van, parking lot, the walls of the high school, and all the surrounding environment, so we could create a clean 2-D image and track it over to replace the telltale rigs. Dereck Sonnenburg did a great job with the 2-D plate work."

A key visual effect was the "sparkle effect" of Edward's skin shining in sunlight when he reveals himself to Bella. "We wanted Edward to look magnificent and stunning and also a little terrifying," Hardwicke said. "It was a challenge, because we've seen a lot of CGI effects, and we [wanted ours to be unique.]"

"It was a very difficult effect," Kidd recalled. "In the book, Edward's skin is described as if it's encrusted with diamonds, but then his skin is described as being smooth, like marble. Literarily it sounds beautiful, but you couldn't create that literally—you can't have a faceted and sparkling look when, at the same time, it's supposed to be smooth. It also had to look smooth without looking as if he had a skin condition. We did a lot of tests with different

"We didn't want Edward's sparkle effect to look blinding, like a diamond. It's the kind of thing that's easy to 'see' on a page, but you have to create something that's an artistic representation of those words. Bella finds it beautiful, but it might frighten someone else. Edward himself is repulsed by it. He says, 'This is the skin of a *killer*.'"

—WYCK GODFREY

Jeanne Van Phue, head makeup artist, touches up Rob.

companies for the sparkle sequence, but Catherine wasn't feeling it. Then ILM became available and were interested in doing the work."

The scene required two components—live-action footage of the actors at a location for the background plate, and the sparkle effect added in postproduction. However, the scheduled shoot at the location was two weeks away and the director hadn't seen any conceptual work for the effect that excited her. Bill George, the storied visual effects supervisor who helmed ILM's work on *Twilight*, recalls the production had "done all the right things." They had shot a test before principal photography of an actor, and had digitally "match moved" sparkle effects, but the various looks weren't working for the director. Time was running out, and Hardwicke told ILM that if she liked the effect she would shoot in close-up, if not, she'd shoot from across the meadow.

"The date for shooting the plate was fast approaching, and it was scary for her, not knowing what the effect would look like and how to cover the sequence," Bill George recalled. "They needed to know the look because that was going to drive the sequence. I've worked on *Star Trek* movies where you have spatial anomalies

> "CATHERINE DESCRIBED THE CHARACTER AS DARKLY MASCULINE. SHE SAID IF THIS MOVIE WAS MADE THIRTY YEARS AGO, EDWARD WOULDN'T BE A VAMPIRE BUT A BIKER, THAT BELLA WOULD BE FALLING IN LOVE WITH A BIKER FROM THE WRONG SIDE OF THE TRACKS."

that could be anything—what does an 'energy ribbon' look like? There's no reference, and I saw this as a similar problem. You want it to look real and seem natural when Edward reveals himself. This is such an important point in the book and the movie. Catherine didn't want it to look like something out of Las Vegas."

George flew up from ILM's San Francisco headquarters to Portland to discuss the look directly with the director and brought along research that showed how certain fish and jellyfish react to light and change color. "I always like to look at the natural world, rather than movies," George noted. "Ultimately, it gave Catherine an education of things that happen naturally in the world, but none of it was *it* for her."

George recalled the director provided a few clues as to what she was looking for. In addition to earlier concept art depicting Edward against a black background, the director kept alluding to the character's inherent darkness. "Catherine described the character as darkly masculine. She said if this movie was made thirty years ago, Edward wouldn't be a vampire but a biker, that Bella would be falling in love with a biker from the wrong side of the tracks."

Hardwicke also wanted to see an animated image, not a still conceptual image. George, working with Mark Casey on the Sabre System, an interactive digital image processing tool, began with a still image of Robert Pattinson and they produced a digital moving effect over the image. "There's this animation of sparkly bits treated like a prism, an optical effect," George explained. "It's the function of the way light hits him, rather than something he is generating. He's not putting off the light, he's reflecting it."

ILM presented the tests to Hardwicke, who was relieved. The look needed finessing, but it was going in the right direction. ILM would develop the final effect in post and she would shoot the live-action plates in close-up. But before they could shoot the outdoor scene, bad weather stole their meadow.

"We had found a meadow at a location at the foothills of Mount Hood that was beautiful and otherworldly, just like it's described in the book," Wyck Godfrey recalled. "This scene was scheduled towards the end of our shooting schedule, when it was closer to spring and we expected to have more moderate weather. But there was an unseasonably long snow season, and right before shooting the location was under four feet of snow. We had only about ten days to find a completely new location, so we were scrambling."

That original meadow location had been found by location scout Don Baldwin, James Lin recalled. "Don had scouted it for *Into the Wild*, which had used it, so we knew the location worked. It wasn't exactly a meadow, but more of a reveal amongst these trees that had a huge boulder that Edward could get up on to

show Bella he was this amazing being. Well, we needed to find another location and sometimes it's better to be lucky than good. Beth and I were having a meal at this restaurant outside Portland and there were rocks on this amazing property surrounding the restaurant, which turned out to be owned by the husband and wife who owned the restaurant. I told Beth, 'You love to scout! Let me know if there's anything good.' I went back to the office and Beth called me about six hours later. She had 300 [digital] images, exclaiming, "Oh my god, this is what we want!" Catherine was so jazzed to hear we had something else, she wanted to see it right away, so Beth showed the photos from that site for Catherine on a monitor at around ten thirty that night."

Although the production team successfully secured a new location for the reveal, the harsh weather that cost them the first site seemed about to take away the second, and with time running out on the shooting schedule. Hardwicke recalls, "We had to have clouds for the entire four-page scene, and when it came time to shoot the reveal—we had a downpour. We nearly gave up, but the downpour broke and we were able to film in the overcast light. Elliot Davis and the electric department created the actual 'sun' with a gigantic Bebe Light."

"It was getting to be six o'clock in the evening, and it was still raining," Godfrey recalled. "If we were going to go over a day, it would have thrown our whole schedule off, since we were so near the end of the movie. Then, just as we were about to call it off, the skies opened [up just enough.] We had an hour to shoot Rob walking in, and get the different angles we needed. So, you can have experiences when you feel the weather's working against you, but then there are those glorious moments when you think, 'Oh my gosh, that had to be divine intervention because we were so screwed without it.'"

*Rob enjoys some rare sun before
the reveal scene was shot.*

"THEN, JUST AS WE WERE ABOUT TO CALL IT OFF,
THE SKIES OPENED [UP JUST ENOUGH.]"

Left to right: Jasper Hale (Rathbone) and Alice Cullen (Greene), Rosalie Hale (Reed) and Emmet Cullen (Lutz), Dr. Carlisle Cullen (Facinelli) and Esme Cullen (Reaser) greet Edward (Pattinson) as he brings Bella (Stewart) home to meet his family.

Rosalie (Reed), Carlisle (Facinelli), and Edward (Pattinson) meet inside the hospital.

Across the bridge over Calawah River, along a winding northern road, and deep in an ancient forest, is the house of the vampires. Bella describes the Cullen house as looking timeless, a structure that sits "tall, rectangular, and well proportioned." Edward, at the wheel of Bella's truck, had turned to her and smiled. "You like it?" In that traditional ritual, Edward had brought her home to meet his family.[10]

Dr. Carlisle Cullen, founder and patriarch of the family, has a philosophy that is more than an espousal of vampire "vegetarianism"—he believes he and his fellows are not monsters but an evolved species. Befitting that exalted view is the Cullen crest, "like a coat of arms that relates to perpetuity and danger and courage," Hardwicke noted. Costume designer Wendy Chuck had the idea of the family crest, and produced initial development drawings which prop master Cynthia Nibler took to completion. Each family member wore the crest in a distinctive, personal way. Rosalie wore her crest as a piece of jewelry on a chain; Alice had a small crest on a ribbon she wore around her neck; Edward, Jasper, and Emmett had their crest set in a leather band that could be worn like a wrist guard; while Dr. Cullen had his set in a ring.

In preproduction, Wendy Chuck proposed to the director that instead of putting the vampires into stereotypical black and dark costumes, they instead go for light and white. "Catherine loved that, going against type. But we had to warm up the whites because of the way the film was being processed in post. So that idea morphed into a palette that was cool blue. Instead of bright and shimmering whites, it got more cream or looked dipped in gray. We found that worked well with their makeup; it made them look more like vampires. The Cullen characters are each very different. A dark blue for Nikki Reed, who plays Rosalie, made her olive skin look more washed out. For Jasper (played by Jackson Rathbone) I kept a Southern influence with jeans and cowboy boots. Alice (Ashley Greene) has a collection of rings and more accessories. The statement for Esme (Elizabeth Reaser) placed her in the 1930s, so her regular look was a high-waisted pencil skirt with a blouse with frills around the neck and a hairstyle that is all very thirties. Dr. Cullen was more timeless, with classical and good quality

EACH FAMILY
MEMBER
WORE THE
CREST IN A
DISTINCTIVE,
PERSONAL
WAY.

"For me, the Cullen world is one of dark and cold. The place where my head was at with the Cullens was they were glacial, like when things get caught in the ice. To me, their world always represented something caught in time. [In their costumes] I always tried to reflect that history, that somehow their lives have all been caught and arrested. That's very much in the book, but that needed to be translated to the screen."

—WENDY CHUCK

clothes. When I was fitting Peter Facinelli for Dr. Cullen, he wanted scarves and shirts with high collars protecting his neck as a character thing because that's the place he was turned, his vulnerable area. We thought that was a great little character point."

In designing a costume for Edward Cullen, Wendy Chuck imagined him as reflective of the Edwardian era, the early decades of the 20th century in which Edward, the mortal, turned into a vampire. That original concept was for well-cut pants and shirts and classical jackets, but evolved into jeans and a more contemporary look. "One of the difficulties with the Cullens was they had to blend with high school kids," Chuck explained. "In the book they're described as rock star gorgeous; they have money and wear designer clothes—and they go to school. They had to not look freakishly different. It became a lot about the fit and the silhouette. So, for example, we put Rob in well-cut jeans and T-shirts and classical lace-up boots. Things evolve as you work on a character. Catherine is very open as a director and also very big on backstory."

The hair department, led by Mary Ann Valdes, faithfully followed the book's description of the characters. "Esme is described as having caramel-colored hair, and we decided to keep her in the 1930s and '40s. It seemed the actors I had all had to be their opposite color. Jackson Rathbone had dark and curly hair and had to be blond. Kellan Lutz, who played Emmett Cullen, had light hair, which had to be darkened. Nikki had dark hair and needed to be blond."

Makeup and hair not only complemented each other, Valdes and makeup artist Jeanne

"Dr. Cullen is described as being blond and almost movie-star-like, so before an actor was cast I researched pictures of classic blond movie stars from the 1930s and '40s. When Peter Facinelli was cast, we colored his normal dark hair blond. It was styled directly back, like he's always running his fingers through it. Hair stays within the basic parameters of a character, but gets tweaked depending on the shots. *Twilight* was very specific, because the look followed the book. But it's no different from working on a period film, where hair and clothes have to be specific but within that parameter you might have street people or aristocrats."

—MARY ANN VALDES

Facinelli and Reaser display their timeless looks.

Hardwicke consults with the good Dr. Cullen.

Van Phue were longtime friends. "We've worked together on many movies," Valdes said. "Because of Jeanne, I met my husband, when she asked me to come to Canada to work with her on *Indian Summer* in 1992 [a '93 release]."

For Jeanne Van Phue, who has been "in the business" for twenty-eight years, *Twilight* marked a return after a forced hiatus. She hadn't worked in nearly two years after suffering a serious knee injury when she tripped over cables and took a nasty fall on *Lords of Dogtown.* "That was my last movie before *Twilight,* and I missed it so much because I love what I do," Van Phue said. "I was bored to tears. I'd never not worked that long in my life. It was making me very sad, not working."

Van Phue had come to Los Angeles from New York, where she had been a hairdresser, but

Edward greets Bella at school on a rare sunny day in Forks, WA.

union regulations forced her to choose between doing hair or makeup. She chose the latter but notes, "I love them both. With makeup you can transform someone, make them look beautiful; you can change the eyebrows and make someone's eyes look bigger. People don't really think of makeup, they don't realize makeup may be covering a blemish or black-and-blue mark. We're trained to make people look better, or older, or stressed out. We do all that! And hair is a big part of the transformation. It's a collaborative effort."

Although Van Phue had Hardwicke's trust and support, other makeup artists were after the *Twilight* assignment—she had to earn her way back. At the outset, the director's only guideline had been to not give the *Twilight* vampires a typical deathly pale look. At that point, Kristen Stewart, Robert Pattinson, and Nikki Reed had been cast, so Van Phue used photographs of the young stars as reference during a whirlwind two-day concept session. Van Phue and Valdes both developed their visions for vampire makeup and hairstyle with artist Kathy Shorkey, who produced a series of illustrations and watercolor paintings that were detailed down to the piercing black eyes with red highlights. "They came out amazing—those drawings got me the job!" Van Phue said. "We got it just right; it was not too pale."

Van Phue also gave Bella a pale cast, just as she is described in the book, accentuating Stewart's fair complexion. As with all makeup assignments, there were weeks of tests to bring to life the vision presented in the concept art. Van Phue experimented with the lightest shades

"THEIR EYES ARE DESCRIBED AS HONEY OR GOLDEN," VAN PHUE EXPLAINED, "BUT WHEN THEY'RE HUNGRY THEY ARE A DARK BROWN AND BLACK, YOU DON'T EVEN SEE THE PUPILS."

The Cullen children in the school cafeteria. Notice that the food remains untouched.

of leading brand names, avoiding any colors that had the slightest warmth. DP Elliot Davis shot tests and, Van Phue recalled, provided his own input ("They look too dead," "They look too human"). The look included contact lenses created by Visioncare in Ventura, with Cristina P. Ceret handpainting each lens. "Their eyes are described as honey or golden," Van Phue explained, "but when they're hungry they are a dark brown and black, you don't even see the pupils. They looked really intense and beautiful. We see Rob twice with the hungry eyes in the school. The rest of the time he has golden eyes."

"ROB LOOKS DIFFERENT FROM THE OTHERS; WE WANTED HIM TO STAND OUT."

Along the way, Van Phue kept detailed notes of every nuance of the work, so that she would be able to duplicate any specific makeup the director wanted for the final look. "I'm making it up as we go! But Catherine likes to see it all and to have you show her everything. She believes in you and is so supportive, which made me want to work all the harder for her."

The hairstyle for Pattinson followed Edward's bronze-colored hair, as described in the novel, a look that also had to work with the pale makeup. "I talked over with Catherine the different shades of bronze hair before I

Charlie gives Edward the policeman's once-over before he allows him to take Bella to the prom.

even met Rob," Valdes said. "His normal hair is like a medium golden brown, and it had been dyed black for a previous movie. The black had faded to a dark color and two inches of his own regrowth had come in and he had two tones going. We had to remove the color from a previous movie to put a new color in it."

In preproduction there was interest in seeing what Edward would look like with long hair. Promotional pictures of the actor had been shot with short hair, and the studio liked the look, but the director wondered what Pattinson's character might look like with long hair. Valdes added glued-in hair extensions to Pattinson, but it was decided the long hair hid his distinctive jawline, so they went back to the shorter look. "If Catherine really liked the long hair, she would talk the studio into it," Valdes said. "The

hair extensions went on that day and we took them out the next day. We all agreed [it should be short]. But Catherine had to see for herself that the short hair was best. If she hadn't seen the longer hair, she'd still be wondering!"

"Edward is the hero, so I had to make him look the best [out] of everyone!" Van Phue noted. "Rob looks drop-dead gorgeous, so I applied his makeup a little thinner. The pale makeup takes life out of you, so I let a tiny bit of his natural skin tone come through. I made his eyes more beautiful and put a little lip stain to make him look appealing. Rob looks different from the others; we wanted him to stand out. But they're all beautiful young people and great actors, not a prima donna among them. They loved each other and they became friends. It was a wonderful set to work on."

The Cullen mansion, in its original owner's state

Catherine Hardwicke put on her architect's hat when it came to the mysterious old house deep in the sheltered rain forest. The novel had described the Cullen house as having south-facing glass walls, a high staircase and high-beamed ceiling, a wooden floor covered with thick white carpets—an elegant home for a clan of wealthy, sophisticated vampires. They found a match in the Portland home of a Nike executive and his family.

Beth Melnick had found the house and had spoken to the executive about letting them use it in the film. Within a couple of weeks, the house was also featured in a magazine called *Portland*

> "THROUGHOUT THE HOUSE, YOU SEE THE EVIDENCE OF ALL THEY MIGHT HAVE LOVED FROM ALL DIFFERENT ERAS."

Spaces, which caught the director's eye. It was a new home set in a forested area, its interior having polished concrete floors and wood and glass surfaces, along with a valuable collection of mid-century modernist furniture. "The owner was a Nike executive and they liked the idea that theirs would be the sophisticated vampire's house," Hardwicke said smiling. "They let us film exteriors and interiors."

The "Nike house," as some referred to the location, was seemingly made-to-order for the Cullen clan. "The interesting thing about the Cullen house location was the walls were stark white, which gave the house a lot of character but also reflected the traditional look of vampires being pale and not getting much sunlight," Phillips noted.

"You actually felt like the home was designed for vampires," Wyck Godfrey added. "One of the rooms upstairs had these double door windows that just opened—there's no deck! I wouldn't feel safe, but for Edward it was a perfect bedroom."

The production still needed to adapt the Nike house to their story needs. For example, neighboring houses were visible, so greenery had to be brought in to block them out and preserve the illusion the Cullen house stood alone in the forest. The art department directed the work, which included an assortment of greenery native to the area, including potted pine trees, the pots concealed with dressings of shrubbery. Gene Serdena added that production design and art direction included many such camouflage uses of greenery, such as hiding wires in scenes where vampires were running through forest.

Another decision was to replace the fabulous furniture, which was deemed not right for the Cullens. Set decorator Serdena noted the "very strong gravitational pull" of the modernism style that would have made it hard for other types of furniture to aesthetically relate. "To these people of great wealth who live forever, a post-modern aesthetic is of little concern," he reflected. "We went with the notion that the Cullens are eclectic and have a rich, wide historical spectrum."

Professional museum movers moved out the furniture for the duration of filming, and the house was transformed with furnishings reflecting both the Cullens' wealth and eclectic taste. "Throughout the house, you see the evidence of all they might have loved from all different eras," Hardwicke noted. "For example, we created Edward's bedroom with old antique radios and all this stuff he's collected in the last ninety years, the evidence of his passion."

Emmet (Lutz) leaps into action to protect Bella.

"There was the idea that these vampires have been around a few hundred years and were able to collect pieces of art. The psychology behind them collecting is they seem to want to remember where they came from, but, at the same time, they know they will live forever. They've moved past the kind of kitsch collecting most people do, and they've each found their niche. Edward's niche, for example, is music. He knows a lot about music and has watched how music has changed over the years, so we tried to create a place for him where there was every piece of musical reproduction equipment, that he likes the idea there's technology to reproduce music. At the same time, the starkness of the house also showed how they'd been able to minimize their lives over the years, particularly so that if they had to leave in an instant, they could. That comes into play towards the end of the movie when they have to leave immediately to go save Bella."

—IAN PHILLIPS

One of the director's ideas when dressing the Cullen house was that as Edward takes Bella up the main staircase she notices what appears to be a piece of abstract wall art—in closer inspection it's comprised of graduation caps they've collected over the decades. "They're nomadic; they matriculate a lot," said Serdena, whose set dressing department created the display. "Bella asks Edward how long he's been seventeen and he says, 'A while.'"

Near the graduation caps is evidence of a special Cullen passion—a display of vintage baseball bats, which alludes to a long relationship with the national pastime. "They play what we call vampire baseball, and [we felt] that said something about the family, the history of Edward and the Cullens," Serdena explained. "What if Edward was a baseball player in the 1920s? We have vintage team baseball photos around [the Cullen house] and there's enough of a suggestion that Edward might be in one of them. Baseball has a longer history for these people than what is on the surface of the film. When we were collecting the different memorabilia, Catherine said, 'I don't think Edward keeps his collection in pristine condition on a shelf.' They become like museum trophies, something that was important to him at one point and then gets shoved on a shelf with a number of objects."

The director came up with another twist on the bedrooms in the house—there are no beds. After all, in Meyer's mythology, vampires never sleep, which leaves plenty of time for brooding, particularly for Edward. "Catherine floated the idea that Edward is desperately lonely and looking for a soul companion and sees that in Bella," Serdena said. "So, maybe the condition of his bedroom is that of someone who's deeply introspective and maybe a little bit lost. We tried to develop that idea, showing his obsessive note taking and pinning things up, piles of journals, philosophy books he's reading and marking passages in during the late nights when he's not sleeping and is devouring information, trying to make sense of what it means to spend eternity walking around and being alone. It's an existential dilemma this character is in, and was an interesting challenge to find a way to bring that into relief within the design of the film.

"We had some interesting discussions," Serdena added. "You start with the notion that when you can live forever, what becomes important to you? What has meaning? I think a vampire, especially Dr. Cullen and other members of the family, are very interested in the passage of time and new things that provide new stimulus to them. In the novel, this is informed by the cars they drive. They like fast, fancy design cars. They're like toys to them. So, let's give them a lot of toys."

"The vampires drive brand-new cars, and we created individual cars appropriate to each character," Phillips said. "We tried to keep their cars spotless to separate them from the rest of the folks in Forks. Edward has a Volvo, Rosalie drives a red convertible, Carlisle has a Mercedes.

"BELLA ASKS EDWARD HOW LONG HE'S BEEN SEVENTEEN AND HE SAYS, 'A WHILE.'"

"THE CULLENS HAVE AN EYE FOR DETAIL AND THEIR AESTHETIC IS SO REFINED THAT EVEN THE DESIGN OF THEIR GARAGE WOULD BE AMAZING."

Emmett drives a Jeep that we kept rather dirty because his character likes to drive deep into the woods. We had our paint department basically create the look of a Jeep that's been through forest and mud."

The Nike house had a conventional two-car garage, but the Cullens needed a bigger space for their fancy cars. A larger garage was found at a private home in another town, but that location also needed additional work to reflect story needs. "The style at the new location was like late 1980s New Wave or what you'd see at the food court at a mall—it was this mishmash of laminated surfaces," Serdena said. "The Cullens have an eye for detail and their aesthetic is so refined that even the design of their garage would be amazing. So we took what existed, this box with doors, and changed it into an ultra-modern, very cool James Bond garage."

The garage also served as a reminder that the Cullens were, like other vampires, nomadic by necessity. "The garage was sort of their place to get really high-tech, but it's also the place that was organized in case they have to leave quickly," Phillips added. "It's there that they keep their emergency supplies, their vampire survival kits, their blood bags, which is basically snack food for the road."

"IT'S THERE THAT THEY KEEP THEIR EMERGENCY SUPPLIES, THEIR VAMPIRE SURVIVAL KITS, THEIR BLOOD BAGS, WHICH IS BASICALLY SNACK FOOD FOR THE ROAD."

Following Hardwicke's philosophy of visually dynamic ways to bring the book alive on screen, the director decided to have the vampires try to cook a meal for Bella. Since they don't eat regular food, it becomes a culinary adventure. "It was a more action-oriented take on the scenario of Edward introducing her to his family," Hardwicke explained.

Elliot Davis noted the production mainly shot on the second floor of the location house. Although the vampires were in their personal domain, the production did not want to overdo the sparkle effect and didn't want to show sunlight—hard to do in a glass house. To avoid the sense of strong sunlit light sources, the cinematography used soft light sources for the house interiors. Because the modern house had open spaces, they also had to be inventive in hiding lights, particularly in the kitchen scene.

THE SEQUENCE, DUBBED "TREE-TO-TREE," FEATURED ANDY CHENG'S WIRE WORK, BUT THERE WAS ONE PROBLEM STRAIGHT OFF—NO TREE OUTSIDE THE WINDOW AT THE LOCATION.

"We set up a big wall of lights on the other side of the house, a big, soft light source, as if ambient light was coming in from that side of the house. I had lights in place behind things. I lit people at the kitchen counter, I hid lights behind ketchup bottles and salt shakers and bowls and things like that. We did have a light outside the kitchen window on what people outside the film business call a 'cherry picker,' a crane with a retractable arm, and we mounted lights on that with a big soft silk in front so the light would come through soft. For Edward's room I put a silk across the whole window and pumped light through it so his room would have this soft light look."

From his bedroom, Edward later takes Bella piggyback on a wild tour of the Cullen house surroundings, beginning with a leap from his window onto a tree. The sequence, dubbed "tree-to-tree," featured Andy Cheng's wire work, but there was

Andy Cheng, front, holding an umbrella, directs Kristen and Rob during the tree-to-tree sequence.

one problem straight off—no tree outside the window at the location. Richard Kidd's visual effects team came to the rescue, supplying a digital tree. Since the shot was planned as a quick cut, they didn't need to create a full CG tree, but could get away with a 2-D still image. "It was actually easier on the stunt people, instead of swinging them by wires and slamming them into a real tree at fullspeed," Kidd noted. "Basically, they jumped out and swung down and made the [body movements] as if they were starting to land on the tree."

Once out of the house, Edward leaps toward the base of another nearby tree and climbs up it. The action featured Kristen Stewart strapped to the back of Robert Pattinson, who was flown on wires. "We had a high line connecting [a series of] trees over the top of the trees, maybe sixty to eighty feet apart," Cheng explained. "From the start at the house, they jump to the next tree and Edward climbs up; they jump and climb, jump and climb. We had cameras on sky cables and helicopters and I was on a descender coming down with a handheld camera."

The romp ends with the sweethearts atop a towering tree providing a stunning view. Location scout Beth Melnick had found a site at the Columbia River Gorge and secured permission to shoot there from the Historic Friends of the Columbia River Gorge. "For [the final vista shot] we found a tree that was sixty to a hundred feet tall atop a thousand-foot cliff," Cheng said. "We had [the actors] climb up and had a safety wire in the tree. After we shot close-ups, I shot two stunt doubles with a helicopter circling the tree as they see the beautiful vista."

The sequence was shot over a four-day period, but the first day was one of the days that became legend on the shoot—there was snow, rain, hail, and sun. "The trees in the sequence are supposed to be green, but that morning, when we went out to shoot, there was snow one-foot deep. The whole mountain was white with snow," Cheng recalled. "I [would have had to] call Catherine and the producers to talk about whether to shoot it white or green, because the weather report [said] it was supposed to snow every day. But that afternoon, the sun came out and all the snow melted."

As Bella becomes friends with the Cullen family, she's honored with an invitation rarely, if ever, accorded a mortal—to be the spectator at a vampire baseball game. Cullen-style ball is played without baseball mitts, barehanded, and the field is twice the size of a sports stadium and set high in the Olympic peaks, where the game is ideally played in a raging thunderstorm. "The primary look for this location was the supernatural aspects of the Cullens—their ability to jump high in the air, and catch a ball," Lin explained. "We had to find a great field set in a natural bowl to sell it with camera angles, a place that seemed primordial. We found it close to the Columbia River Gorge, looking off the walls of the Gorge."

Emblematic of the Cullens' passion for the game were their retro baseball caps and outfits. The costume department used vintage uniforms for fitting purposes, and then created multiples (six to twelve per person, Wendy Chuck estimates), because of the punishment the outfits would take as actors and stunt doubles ran,

As Bella becomes friends with the Cullen family, she's honored with an invitation

RARELY, IF EVER, ACCORDED A MORTAL—TO BE
THE SPECTATOR AT A VAMPIRE BASEBALL GAME.

jumped, and slid at the rugged location. The ball game was scheduled soon after the dance studio fight that opened the schedule, a time when the weather was still particularly harsh. "It was scheduled for three days of first unit and three days of second unit," Hardwicke explained. "Because of weather problems we had less than two days of first unit shooting time."

Chuck recalls that just getting to the remote baseball game location from the production's base camp was an adventure, a thirty to forty minute drive by transportation van along a muddy one-lane road. "The weather was absolutely the worst—it was rain and cold *together*. I kept saying rain boots, rain boots, rain boots, cold, cold, cold. You can prepare for it, but it's nothing like being there. When we got to the meadow to do the baseball game, it was miserable. It didn't matter how many layers of clothing, everyone was cold and damp. You could stand it for thirty minutes, but people were out there twelve to fourteen hours a day. The actors wore thermal underwear underneath their costumes, but deep into the shoot the warm underclothes of choice became the thin type of scuba suits that surfers wear, [because] they worked the best. I laid out scuba suits with their costumes every day."

The baseball game was a major sequence for the visual effects department. The visual effects supervisor worked with the CIS Vancouver effects house on "sky replacement" shots, which, as the term implies, involves digitally substituting skies shot on location with digitally image processed ones that serve the sequence's aesthetic demands, including lightning effects. They qualified these shots as "invisible effects,"

Richard Kidd noted, as they were designed to not be obviously fantastical but fit in seamlessly and naturally. The visual effects department had to create another clean plate for sky replacement work, and, since the changing weather and seasons made it prohibitive to return, they also needed an image of the entire location so they could have a digital background for any potential greenscreen work in case the production needed re-shoots of the location. The solution was a "giga-pixel image," with the visual effects work aided by Eric Hanson, a leading expert on giga-pixel imagery.

The ball game was an opportunity to see the vampires cut loose from their normal reserve when blending into the human world. To DP Elliot Davis, there was also the necessity for shooting the game "like a highlight reel," focusing on hitting, running, fielding, and sliding. "We tried to make the game as kinetic as possible. I told Catherine the action should be ramped up, speeding things up and slowing them down. This would provide some 'shock and awe' for Bella, since the movie is supposed to be seen from her point of view. The ramping effect would also reflect her heightened senses as she's having her mind blown, to feel what she's feeling, as she watches these vampires play."

The Crazy Horse Rig, tested in preproduction, was an invaluable tool for the ramping effect. As planned, the dual-mounted and mirrored cameras with the beam splitter allowed for filming of the same angle at different frame speeds for pitching and hitting. "We wanted to switch, in postproduction editing, from the point of view of the baseball coming in to the batter in real time and then pushing into slow

motion as the bat hits the ball," Kidd explained. "That way we could get the feeling of slo-mo and then speed it up instantaneously."

The thrill of vampire baseball is the titanic force of hits, bullet throws, the super speed at which outfielders go after balls. The visual effects team created computer-generated baseballs, including replacement CG balls for the illusion of outfielders catching the speeding balls in their bare hands. Actors in the outfield would palm a small plastic stand-in ball that was virtually invisible to the camera, but allowed the performers to not only pretend to make a catch but realistically grip and close their fingers around a stand-in ball that would then be replaced in postproduction with the CG ball.

There would also be real baseballs flying at super-speed thanks to what Andy Weder called a "baseball launcher." A big steel tube, like an air motor, was loaded with balls (greased with Vaseline to make the tight fit) that were shot one at a time out of the tube at the rate of 150 pounds of pressure per square inch. For the illusion of base runners sliding along base paths at super-normal lengths and speeds, the special effects unit had a trench dug and laid with about twenty feet of Plexiglas that was slicked up with shuffleboard wax and concealed with a layer of dirt.

Cheng's unit provided major wire work

for the sequence. Rob Pattinson, for example, showed off Edward's great speed in real time with a cable moving him across the field at thirty feet a second (the average vampire, Cheng notes, runs at twenty feet a second). "When he ran, we traveled with him," Cheng said. "For the baseball game we had a high line which was one hundred feet high and a thousand feet long, and we had a track and like a skateboard [atop the overhead line] with a half-inch wire that came down and attached to the actor [via a hidden harness the actor wore]. We had a winch, like a motor, and we'd computer program it to move at twenty feet a second, fifty feet a second, or whatever we wanted, and maintain that speed while attached to the actor or stunt double. They looked like they were really running, but their feet are barely touching the ground as they maintain the speed of twenty feet or fifty feet every second. The same for jumping. It's the same high line, just lifting up and they have a curve, instead of running—that was a computer setup, too. We, of course, had tested to make sure of what we could do and not do."

As in the book, the baseball game is interrupted by the arrival of nomadic vampires. Unlike Dr. Cullen's sophisticated coven, these wanderers have no compunction about doing what normal vampires do best when it's time to feed.

Elemental Forces

*Kristen and Taylor share a soggy
moment during filming.*

Edward arrives at Forks High School, wary of contact with Bella.

In a scene Andy Cheng's second unit filmed for the beginning of the movie, a deer is chased through the woods while Bella Swan contemplates in voice-over what it would be like to die and be reborn as a vampire and spend eternity with the one she loves. "The deer is being chased and it gets caught—you see it's Edward," Cheng explained. "We had a cable camera on top of the trees parallel with the camera chasing the deer. Visual effects then combined Edward, making it look like he's caught the deer."

When Edward hungers, he and his brethren hunt wild game. The Cullens have grown accustomed to this diet, but it's an acquired taste. Deep inside, their repressed vampire instinct hungers for human fare. In Meyer's novel, when Edward tells Bella the story of Carlisle Cullen's conversion to vampire vegetarianism, he puts it in heroic terms. Carlisle, a native born Londoner in the 1640s, was the son of a persecutor of Roman Catholics whose crusade against vampires ironically led to Carlisle being caught by one of the undead and turned. Mortified he had become a monster, he went into hiding and fought the hunger. Growing weaker, finally overcome by the fresh need to feed, he attacked some passing deer—and discovered that satisfied him. It was a revelation. He had feasted on venison in his former life; he could do so now. Cullen swam from England across the Channel to France, where he roamed the continent, living a nocturnal existence that allowed him to consort with humans and avoid the sun. He studied art and music, but found his "penance," as Edward called it, learning medicine and saving human life. By force of will he mastered his predatory desires, and eventually the sight and scent of human blood did not drive him to vampiric bloodlust. A chosen few he saved from certain death to make his own, and he taught them his philosophy. "I can't adequately describe the struggle; it took Carlisle two centuries of torturous effort to perfect his self-control," Edward tells Bella in the novel. "Now he is all but immune to the scent of human blood, and he is able to do the work he loves without agony." [11]

Laurent, Victoria, and James, the nomadic vampires who interrupt the Cullens on their playing field, end one game, but another, deadlier game begins—James, revealed to be the leader of his coven, is a tracker and eager for the sport of claiming Bella, while the Cullens

James (Gigandet) awaits Bella in Phoenix, AZ.

Meyer's world, the only way to kill a vampire is not through the hoary technique of pounding a stake through the heart, but from tearing them to bits and burning the pieces.

The merciless hunter knows the vulnerability of his prey and goes after Bella's weak point—her mother. Thus, *Twilight* leaves the stormy world of the Pacific Northwest for the sunny Southwest. Bella has resolved to meet her end in order to save her mother, who is being held hostage by James. Bella slips away from her vampire protectors to meet her destiny at a place that recalls earlier times—Mimi's School of Dance, the dance studio near her mother's house where James awaits her arrival.

For the production, the return to Phoenix and Scottsdale was accomplished by shooting in the southern California town of Valencia, which had the requisite dry and arid look. However, the exterior for the dance studio was an empty brick building in Portland with arched windows that Ian Phillips recalls had formerly been an upholstery company. The building itself dates back to the early 1900s and was built like a large warehouse that forms two floors inside. However, the production imagined the interior space as only one story, to take advantage of the large, arched windows they could match on an interior set.

The *Twilight* construction crew built the studio interior in a Portland warehouse. It was the finale in terms of storyline but, due to actor availability, was the first item on the shooting schedule. The design of the big scene would evoke one of the classic sets and scenes in the hard-boiled annals of film *noir*.

Director Orson Welles's Hall of Mirrors sequence in *The Lady from Shanghai* is one of the greatest movie climaxes. A deadly triangle between a seaman (played by Welles), a crippled and ruthless lawyer (Everett Sloane), and the lawyer's sexy, devious wife (Rita Hayworth) all have a final showdown in the mirrored room of a San Francisco oceanfront amusement park where guns are drawn and accounts settled. Only one survives after the guns have been emptied and the Fun House glass shattered. Welles's famous scene has often been imitated, notably in a battle filmed in a mirrored chamber at the climax of Bruce Lee's classic martial arts adventure *Enter the Dragon*.

Lady from Shanghai and *Enter the Dragon*

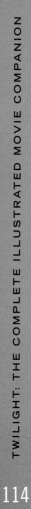

inspired Catherine Hardwicke's approach to the
dance studio where James corners Bella, and the
subsequent battle when Edward arrives to save his
true love. It would be a mirrored space, from wall
mirrors to mirrors on pillars. To avoid reflecting camera or crew, each individual mirror was
hinged so they could be rotated by hand, up or
down, or left to right, allowing for the design of
specific shooting angles to avoid reflections. Even
the mirrored pillar could be rotated around.

"The action scenes were the most demand-
ing in terms of multiples for costumes," Wendy
Chuck noted. "As fate would have it, the biggest
challenges for my department—the big fight
at the dance studio and the baseball game—all
came at the beginning of the shoot, at the same

time. The first three weeks, we had to shoot
them first."

The showdown at the dance studio was a
major sequence for stunt coordinator and second
unit director Cheng. He knew in advance the
dimensions of the set so that, as it was being
built, he could mark it out with tape in a
rehearsal space and begin rehearsing the fight
and wire flying setups. It was ironic that snow
was still outside while the dance studio set represented a location in hot and arid Arizona. But
it had been a risk starting the filming schedule
with the movie's big finish, a violent sequence
that would see glass surfaces shattered and
mirrored pillars and floor smashed. If the lead
actors had gotten hurt, it would have stopped

"For the fight, we had to figure out what it would look like. Catherine and I ended up calling it 'animal style.' The idea was the good vampire, Edward, is not violent; he doesn't want to fight, until James [threatens Bella]—that turns him crazy. [They become] very violent, they bite like an animal. We watched videotapes of tigers, how they lunge and attack, how a panther runs. We did the research, then [artists] storyboarded the fight, and shot a rehearsal to show Catherine and the producers. I shot rehearsals with a handi-cam, but the actual scene used five cameras. It wasn't planned to be shot in one take. We did not shoot a master—I picked the best angles, [and] I divided up the sequence for a specific punch and kick. At the best editing point, I cut to a better angle. We shot dozens of setups, but how it looks depends on the final edit."

—ANDY CHENG

the show. "It was kind of scary, because I had to have a good, exciting sequence," Cheng said.

The construction department built the interior set, but Tyan Bardon and Dean Roberts of the special effects unit saw to the building of the breakaway floor, which looked like a real hardwood surface but was lightweight balsa wood. Some brickwork in the studio was made of soft plaster, while breakaway mirrors were made of "Pico-Tech," from Alfonso's Breakaway Glass company. "They used to call it 'candy glass,' but instead of sugar and stuff it's made out of a weak plastic," Weder explained. "You then mirror one side, which can look a little wavy, but you're not dwelling on the mirror for very long."

Elliot Davis and Andy Cheng worked together to break down the sequence and make sure every shot was a seamless match from first unit to second unit. When Davis's first unit filmed with the lead actors they also had to make sure they matched the look of scenes that might have specific wreckage from Cheng's stunt and fight work. "For the studio it was supposed to be night in there, so I kind of made it a netherworld time," Davis added. "I used harsh lights, which [were] unfiltered, without silks."

Andy Cheng's stunt team flew stunt doubles to give the effect of Edward and James slamming each other around the studio. The wires could go through holes in a moveable ceiling to overhead rigging or, if the ceiling didn't need to be in a shot, could be slid open.

"It was great to do a movie with so many physical effects, but Andy Cheng pulled off a lot of the miracles with his flying team," Weder noted. "The most common rig was an overhead cable system to fly up and down on winches and controlled by computer, with the operator, Kevin Chase, on the button. They rehearsed with weighted sand bags first, then put the actor at half speed and built up to it. A lot was also, as Andy likes to say, 'Hong Kong style,' where they're manually pulled offstage. Some of his best stuff was in the fight sequence, slamming people on the floor and smashing into the mirrors. Slamming them into the breakaway floor was soft and easy, but it was when they ran into each other, and head-butted each other, that we had to switch out guys after a while."

The violent scene included a terrifying moment when James attacks Bella and draws blood. But other than a bite effect provided by second makeup artist Rolf Kebbler (an "out of kit" compound for the bite mark, with a dash of movie blood), it was a rare bit of bloodletting. "How many vampire movies do you know where you hardly shoot nights, and there's hardly any blood?" Weder rhetorically asked.

THE QUILEUTE INDIAN TRIBE, THEIR ONCE VAST TRIBAL LANDS REDUCED TO THE NARROW BORDERS OF THEIR RESERVATION ALONG THE PACIFIC OCEAN, INCLUDES LA PUSH BEACH—AND IS OFF-LIMITS TO "THE COLD ONES," AS THE CULLENS ARE KNOWN TO THE TRIBE.

In the *Twilight* world, strange secrets lurk beneath the surface. The Quileute Indian tribe, their once vast tribal lands reduced to the narrow borders of their reservation along the Pacific Ocean, includes La Push Beach—and is off-limits to "the cold ones," as the Cullens are known to the tribe. It's an old truce between vampires and their opposites, as Jacob Black shares with Bella in a whispered story of the ancient enmity between vampires and werewolves.

Tribal elder Billy Black wore a jacket that did not fit the designed color palette, but the director had allowed for an exception because she liked the red and gray fleece jacket that actor Gil Birmingham brought in, which had the vibe of the Northwest and was decorated with Native American designs. Costume designer Wendy Chuck got into the Native American aspects of the film later in the production when the Quileute beach scenes were filmed.

Chuck's research included a trip to Seattle to photograph Native Americans there. But it was Solomon Trimble, a part Quileute Indian who plays Jacob's friend in the film, who was a font of information during his fitting sessions

Bella (Stewart) and Jacob (Lautner) get to know each other and swap stories on the shores of the reservation at La Push.

Left: Charlie (Burke) and Billy (Birmingham) catch up.
Right: Jacob Black (Lautner) and friends from the tribe.

with the costume designer. "He blew my mind; he was like an anthropologist. He was learning the Quileute language and had made a drum and was composing songs in the language as he learned it. The Quileute tribe has less of a sustainable economy. The kids mostly fish and hang out, they wear T-shirts with Native pride slogans, or they'll get a big Sharpie and make their own T-shirts with Native pride words mixed with hip-hop, or an image from an old photograph of Native Americans on horses with rifles. I do my research; I wanted to get it right. But I got an education from Sam. He came in wearing jeans and a tank top and Western boots and a great jacket that looked very Northwest, and he'd tell me about things he had. The next time he came in, he brought a big long coat his mother had made out of a blanket that happened to have a wolf on the back."

The Oregon coast provided the beach scenes in which Bella and her friends meet Jacob, Sam, and some of the other young Quileute Indians. The beach scenes not only marked the end of production filming but the worst weather the production faced. "The scene on the beach went down in our collective history as the worst day for our whole crew," Wendy Chuck noted.

That worst day was a Tuesday of the last week in Oregon, Hardwicke recalled. The park service didn't allow vehicles on the beach, so all the equipment had to be carried down to the shooting location. Makeup artist Jeanne Van Phue recalls that to get down to the shooting spot on the beach, they had to walk across smooth, slippery rocks deposited over time by the crashing waves to a height of fifteen to twenty feet. For Elliot Davis and his camera crew it was impossible to get cables down, so they used available light and bounce cards, with a battery-operated "sun gun" to shine a little light in actors' faces. "For the story, we wanted it cloudy, but it was really rainy and cold," Davis recalled. "But you have to be like the mailman—you have to deliver."

This was also the day Stephenie Meyer and her husband and two of their young sons came to visit, as well as some media people. "The worst

"THE SCENE ON THE BEACH WENT DOWN IN OUR COLLECTIVE HISTORY AS THE WORST DAY FOR OUR WHOLE CREW," WENDY CHUCK NOTED.

day of our whole lives was the beach," Van Phue exclaimed. "My husband [John W. Murphy, dolly grip on the show] has been doing this as long as I have and he said it was his most miserable day on a movie set *ever*. There was cold, sleet, and rain. It was miserable; I'd never been that unhappy in my life! My legs weren't a hundred percent because of my knee surgery, and they told me not to do it. But I said, 'This is my job and I really need to be there.' I still made it to every location and I

Actors Justin Chon (Eric) and Christian Serratos (Angela), along with the crew, wait out the weather.

walked that beach. We got through it."

Catherine Hardwicke noted that day they faced "extreme weather" conditions the likes of which her veteran crew had never experienced. She recalls the "hell" of that shooting day:

"First, the crew bus was slowed down for an hour driving through a snowstorm on a mountain road. Then, the equipment had to be hauled by hand down a rocky beach. Then it rained nonstop—freezing, forty-five-degree-angle rain. The camera crew, clad head-to-toe in Gore-Tex, wrapped the camera bodies completely in plastic and we tried to shoot anyway. But water leaked in and destroyed the Steadicam monitor, followed by the watery death of a second, brand-new monitor. George Billinger, our Boy Scout Steadicam operator, had a third monitor still in the box, and the show went on.

"Finally, we got four takes of the master Steadicam shot in the pouring rain. Kristen was wearing a raincoat, my gloves, my tall boots, and a wet suit underneath to keep warm. Then we shot one take of Jacob's single and the downpour stopped. We then had to rush and shoot one take of the master and one take of Bella without the rain so that all the shots would match. Of course, by the time we got to the establishing shot it was raining again and the tide had come up. We barely got a version of the first scene— and that was just the first half of the day!

"Now the crew had to hike back across the rocks with their equipment in the pouring rain, which took an hour and a half, to find a lunch tent that was literally blowing away. The crew and various [of the visiting] reporters had to hold it down. Meanwhile, the nearly horizontal freezing rain continued and I was told I had to shoot the beach surf scene anyway. So I found some of the local extras' surf vans and arranged them in the parking lot to block the wind and had Bella and Angela play the scene sitting in the van. It was miserable and many of the crew complained about 'inhuman conditions.' But we got the scene...barely. The next day, one of the producers congratulated me on making the day, saying, 'No other director that I know would have kept shooting in those conditions.' I was thinking: 'You mean I had a choice?'"

Such days pass into legend among film crews. Wendy Chuck recalls some of them huddling to exchange war stories, and it was nearly unanimous this was everyone's worst day on a movie set. "We thought nobody could top it as our worst day ever. The only one was the first A.D. [assistant director], who once

Kristen Stewart and Christian Serratos shoot their scene in the van, during the cold rain.

"The weather absolutely became a character in this movie. We couldn't control it and we had to be fully prepared to change locations and move quickly if the weather got really bad. It made for some tense times, not knowing what was going to happen. Sometimes it would be raining, or there'd be hail and sleet. But people worked through it. You just had to forge ahead."

—IAN PHILLIPS

was working on one of those extreme mountaineering movies and was stuck in a tent on a mountain in a blizzard, waiting to be rescued by helicopter, and nearly died! He was the only person who topped it."

Chuck recalls she didn't have to be on set the whole day, and had headed back to base camp, a forty-five-minute drive away. When she got to camp, which was set up in a parking lot on the coastline, she looked north, back toward the shooting location. "There was this huge, big rainy cloud just hanging over the beach and the location set. And it stayed there all day."

By the last night of shooting, May 2, 2008, a downpour soaked through layers of that protective garb Catherine Hardwicke had

bought with the assurance they would keep her dry. Hardwicke's production diary report on the *Twilight* Web site that last night had the weary resolution of a dispatch from a long siege: "Principal photography is ending…we survived snow, hail, sleet, torrential downpours, and blazing sun (when we didn't want it)—sometimes all in one day. SEVERE WEATHER is an understatement."

But the day before they wrapped, Hardwicke drew positive energy from the sight of a group of Twilighters, some of whom had come all the way from Arizona to catch a glimpse of filming. "I was bone tired, but that revved me up to see how much you guys care," Hardwicke noted on her final Web site communiqué.[12]

126

"The first piece {Carter Burwell} wrote is the Bella and Edward love theme, or 'Bella's Lullaby.' It ends on a beautiful piano piece, which the crazy-talented Rob Pattinson actually plays on camera."

T wilight postproduction was crunch time for the director, for editor Nancy Richardson (who now had massive amounts of footage to deal with), for Richard Kidd's visual effects work, for composer Carter Burwell (who was providing the musical score), and for other departments—a lot of work to do in the months before the theatrical release date. To put the film's fast-track schedule in perspective, from the time Catherine Hardwicke first looked through potential screenplays at Summit and found the early *Twilight* script, to its release in theaters, just under two years would have passed.

In mid-July, the halfway point of postproduction, Hardwicke made a state-of-the-film appraisal:

"For the first week of the editing process, I was devastated. Wrecked. Heartbroken about all the shots I didn't get. I had envisioned so much more wonderful stuff—but the weather and other elements did not always cooperate. I finally 'sucked it up' and started appreciating what we did accomplish and tried to make it work the best we could. It's a crazy Rubik's Cube: How can you put these pieces together to tell the most potent story? Nancy Richardson, our editor, is incredible at looking through dailies and selecting the most delicious bits and putting together a great, watchable sequence very, very quickly. At the end of each day, she would have cut the scenes from the day before and put great [temporary] music and sound effects—I could instantly see how things were working. From then on, we have been constantly trying new ideas, new combinations, refining and polishing. We've got all these elements to work with: visual effects, music, ADR [additional dialogue recording] lines, sound effects—hopefully the postproduction team jumps onboard and everyone just keeps elevating it. Working with our composer, Carter Burwell, on the score, is a pleasure. We've been editing the film with temp score (some from Carter's old movies), but the exciting part is when Carter creates themes just for our film. The first piece he wrote is the Edward and Bella love theme, or 'Bella's Lullaby.' It ends on a beautiful piano piece, which the crazy-talented Rob Pattinson actually plays on camera."

As a rough cut came together, the final film took shape. Producer Godfrey, who believed in the visceral feeling of shooting in real locations, concluded that that aspect had added an intangible *something* to the mix. Some of that manic energy of rushing around to get a shot seemed to have seeped into the fabric of the film, reflecting the heightened state of young love and Bella's and Edward's chaotic emotions. "If you needed the rain and it started raining again, you'd have to run back; it was about keeping enough cameras and setups going. It was crazy, like film school, just running around and grabbing it. But after seeing the film, it provided an energy, a heightened awareness."

Visual effects supervisor Richard Kidd was seeing to the completion of all the elements involving digital enhancement, including the sparkle effect for Edward's reveal, which Industrial Light & Magic was taking from concept to completion.

The first step in finalizing the effect was when Robert Pattinson visited

Gentle Giant Studios, a 3-D scanning company in Burbank, and a full head and body scan was taken of the actor. "We got that scan back as a data cloud, basically a model of the surface of his skin," ILM supervisor Bill George explained. "We used the body scan as a very accurate model of him and rigged it so we could move it with him. This CG model was match-moved to his action, so we had like a ghost image over the top of him, with the sparkly bits able to move with his skin. You only see the effect on the sunlit side, and we also added shards of light to the scene."

The last part of the process, when the film was finally edited together, was to balance the color and produce the final look of the film. It was an integral part of filmmaking, as scenes shot out of sequence needed to match color continuity, and was also an artistic tool for giving a film a final tone and texture. "I view the look of this film as very desaturated, a cool, pale tone, which reflects the Pacific Northwest," noted Elliot Davis, who helmed the color correction work. "This was

"I VIEW THE LOOK OF THIS FILM AS VERY DESATURATED, A COOL, PALE TONE, WHICH REFLECTS THE PACIFIC NORTHWEST," NOTED ELLIOT DAVIS.

the cool range of color throughout the movie. I punch the greens up to accentuate the lushness and crush the blacks to give it a reference. We make sure skin tones are the same. Every scene is corrected the way we want to see it. An interesting thing was how naturally pale Kristen Stewart's skin was. It was very much like the way Bella is described as being pale in the book. She seemed to belong with the vampire clan; it was like she was already a vampire herself!"

Producer Greg Mooradian, one of the first outside the walls of Little, Brown and Company to see the potential in that original raw *Twilight* manuscript, had followed its course from unknown factor to publishing phenomenon to movie property and finished motion picture. He had seen Meyer grow into a major voice who became hands-on in the movie's development. "She really is the franchise," he said.

For Meyer it had been an unexpected roller-coaster ride that kept building to the movie's opening, from the release of the first teaser trailer to a July 18 *Entertainment Weekly* cover article (with stars Pattinson and Stewart featured on the cover, Stewart holding the "forbidden love" motif of a red apple), which likened her and her work to J. K. Rowling and the Harry Potter series. From her dream of June 2, 2003, to the November 21, 2008, release of the movie adaptation had been fewer than five years.

Mooradian had heard the story about the dream that started it all, that sleeping vision of the young girl and the handsome vampire having their intense conversation. But what struck him was how unplanned Stephenie Meyer's literary success had been. "I asked Stephenie if this had been something she was building towards, whether she was just waiting for the right moment. She said, 'No, no.' She told me she had never longed to be a novelist before this and was sort of awaiting her muse. The dream literally woke her up and made her decide she wanted to write [this story]. Just imagine, at that stage of your life! What a strange thing. It makes *me* wonder what tomorrow is going to bring…"

Meanwhile, in the *Twilight* movie world, sets had been struck, crew members had headed on to other projects, the massive paper flow of screenplays and call sheets and crew lists were being filed away or dropped into recycling bins, production office numbers were being deleted or disconnected. This band of filmmakers had come together for a time, and each had moved on, leaving a movie, and personal memories, in their wake.

"It's like a big, crazy family," Hardwicke mused. "Over the course of six months and two hundred fifty people, the family dynamics can swing from highly functional to depressingly dysfunctional. With some family members, you

Left to right: Hardwicke, Stewart, Meyer, and Rob Friedman, Co-Chairman and CEO of Summit, Entertainment take a break on the set.

can't wait to say good-bye; others you miss dearly. I lived for those creative jam sessions talking to Elliot Davis about cool shots, or with actors about their characters. Crew members would bring inspiring films, photographs, artwork, and music. Our storyboard artists, Phil Keller and Trevor Goring, had some killer ideas. Patrick Smith, my assistant, straight out of NYU film school, could always come up with a 'hip fast song for the prom in the next twenty minutes,' or the coolest shoes for Edward to play baseball in. The assistant director team was particularly collaborative: Jamie Marshall, our co-producer and first assistant director, and Michael 'Viggs' Vigglietta [2nd unit first A.D.] and Andy Cheng would work crazy hours dreaming up great stuff and scouting locations. Second unit came back with improbably exotic shots of untrained deer galloping through the forest and stunt doubles nearly getting blown off one-hundred-twenty-foot trees by the helicopter backdraft—but they always got the shot! Our stars, Rob and Kristen, both had great ideas about music—Rob has recorded several songs for the film and Kristen suggested the final prom song, by Iron and Wine."

The film, as in the book, ends with Bella making it to the Forks High School prom. It was no high school gym dance—the prom is held at

"OUR STARS, ROB AND KRISTEN, BOTH HAD GREAT IDEAS ABOUT MUSIC — ROB HAS RECORDED SEVERAL SONGS FOR THE FILM AND KRISTEN SUGGESTED THE FINAL PROM SONG, BY IRON AND WINE."

ENOUGH FOR FOREVER

131

a 1920s inn and the young people dance under the cover of an outdoor gazebo. The sequence was filmed by the Columbia Gorge, which made for breathtaking views. It was near the end of the schedule, in late April, but freezing cold and snowing. But the dancing went on.

Andy Weder recalls that when he was up for the job of *Twilight* special effects supervisor, his daughter Chelsea told him, "You *have* to get this job!" He did, and it was Chelsea who had a coveted cameo as one of the prom dancers who leaves the floor to Edward and Bella. Choreographer Dee Dee Anderson provided direction to Pattinson and Stewart on their waltz moves.

For the romantic touch that ends the movie, the special effects department used what Weder likens to a gigantic record player turntable that could spin the dancers in circles, which they had gotten from Special Effects Unlimited, a venerable L.A. rental house. The final section, including a piece built by the construction department, made for a ten-foot-diameter

Charlie Swan can't help but smile to see his girl Bella as she makes her entrance for Edward before they leave for the prom

CATHERINE HARDWICKE NOTED THAT FOR
ALL THE INHERENT DARKNESS THAT CAME
WITH VAMPIRES, IT WAS THE LOVE STORY THAT
TOUCHED PEOPLE.

For all the dreams and development, the manic schedule, harsh weather conditions, and creative jam sessions, the whole movie-making journey—the *Twilight* dream coalesced in the director's mind to a single image from the shoot, a tableau of the young girl and the vampire who is forever seventeen.

"Our last scene was a night on a cold, dark mountain road—Edward and Bella were driving in the truck. Under that crisp moon, it was like they were in their own brightly lit bubble. It made me so sad to think it would be the last [scene] Edward and Bella would be in together.

"People have asked 'what category' the film would be. Someone who saw it said it was a gothic horror romance with comedy! But I like that it doesn't fit in [a category]. It's a coming-of-age story; it's got dark humor. I hope the film appeals to romantics, but it's a scary movie, too. It gets pretty badass at the end—the fight scenes are pretty terrifying. So, hopefully, an audience will feel a lot of emotions. Actually, I want [someone who's seen the movie] to grab their boyfriend or girlfriend and go and make out, then turn around and go back and see the movie again, then make out again! [laughs]"

turntable built into the dance floor. "We could control how fast it went," Weder explained. "The camera operator could stand on it, they did a lot of handheld and Steadicam camera work. We wouldn't show the floor itself spinning. Catherine had asked for this effect; she thought it would add a romantic and magical feel as [they filmed] Edward and Bella dancing."

Catherine Hardwicke noted that for all the inherent darkness that came with vampires, it was the love story that touched people. Even her mother, in her seventies, had been taking art classes and was thinking of switching to biology to see if she could get a lab partner like Edward, she notes. "People of all ages are looking for a perfect love. People have read these books and been inspired to get out there!"

"ACTUALLY, I WANT [SOMEONE WHO'S SEEN THE MOVIE] TO GRAB THEIR BOYFRIEND OR GIRLFRIEND AND GO AND MAKE OUT, THEN TURN AROUND AND GO BACK AND SEE THE MOVIE AGAIN, THEN MAKE OUT AGAIN!"

NOTES

1: Stephenie Meyer, *Twilight* (New York: Megan Tingley Books, Little Brown and Company, paperback edition, 2006), pp. 232–233.

2: Ibid., p. 343.

3: Emily W. Sunstein, *Mary Shelley: Romance and Reality* (Baltimore, Maryland: The John Hopkins University Press, 1989), p. 122.

4: Introductory essay by John Mason Brown; Robert Louis Stevenson, *Strange Case of Dr. Jekyll and Mr. Hyde* (New York: The Heritage Press, 1952), p. x.

5: Bio material and direct quotes from Stephenie Meyer Web site, "Unofficial Bio" and "The Story Behind *Twilight*," http://www.stepheniemeyer.com.

6: Barbara E. Horst, *Unholy Hungers: Encountering the Psychic Vampire in Ourselves & Others* (Boston: Shambhala, 1996), pp. 34 – 35; Byron and "the vampire image" from: David J. Skal, *Hollywood Gothic: The Tangled Web of Dracula from Novel to Stage to Screen* (New York: W.W. Norton & Company, 1990), p. 13.

7: Joel Schumacher commentary on *The Lost Boys* DVD, disc one, 19 minute mark.

8: Mark Cotta Vaz and Craig Barron, *The Invisible Art: The Legends of Movie Matte Painting* (San Francisco: Chronicle Books, 2002), pp. 163, 175.

9: Meyer, *Twilight* paperback, p. 5.

10: Ibid., p. 321.

11: Ibid., pp. 339 – 340.

12: "That's a Wrap," 5:46 pm, Friday, May 2, 2008, *Twilight* movie Web site, http://greetingsfromtwilight.com.

ACKNOWLEDGMENTS

◄◄ ►►

My thanks to editor Joe Monti, who asked me if I wanted to visit the *Twilight* world. Writing this book was a formidable task, but accomplished largely due to the superb efforts of Sabryna Phillips at Summit, who coordinated the interviews. This book wouldn't have happened without her, nor would it have happened without the amazing support of the filmmakers who shared their insights. A tip of the hat and a low bow as well to Catherine Hardwicke, who gave of her time even while she was deep into postproduction. I'm also thankful for those who arranged other interviews and connections: Patrick Smith at Catherine Hardwicke's office, Emmy Castlen at Sunswept Entertainment, and Stephen Kenneally at ILM. My deepest appreciation to my agent, John Silbersack, who gave his usual superb effort on my behalf, and his assistant, Libby Kellogg, who is always of good cheer and on top of things. A hug all around to my family, with love to my mother, who proofed my manuscript with her usual keen eye. To Mike Wigner, the world's greatest bicycle messenger—see you at Vesuvio's. And a fond hello to Gretchen Young, who helped facilitate my *Twilight* connection.

AUTHOR'S CREDITS

Mark Cotta Vaz is a *New York Times* bestselling author with twenty-six published books. His works include the classic film history *The Invisible Art: The Legends of Movie Matte Painting* (co-authored with Academy of Motion Picture Arts and Sciences Board of Governors member Craig Barron), which won best-book awards from the Theatre Library Association (TLA) of New York and the United States Institute of Theatre Technology. His critically acclaimed biography *Living Dangerously: The Adventures of Merian C. Cooper, Creator of* King Kong, was a *Los Angeles Times* bestseller and TLA finalist selection. His "making of" books have documented the first season of *Lost* and such feature film productions as *Spider-Man*, *Spider-Man 2*, and *The Spirit*.

The phenomenon continues....

STEPHENIE MEYER

the twilight saga:
the official guide

You may think you already know everything there is to know about the unforgettable world Stephenie Meyer created in *Twilight*, *New Moon*, *Eclipse*, and *Breaking Dawn*, but this essential edition—the only official guide—will put your knowledge to the test! With character profiles, genealogical charts, maps, extensive cross-references, and much more, this comprehensive handbook is a must-have for every Twilight Saga fan.

Check www.stepheniemeyer.co.uk for details.

Little, Brown Book Group
Hachette Livre UK